FRIEND OF GOD STUDY GUIDE

FRIEND OF GOD STUDY GUIDE

Discussing and applying the message of Abraham today

John C. Lennox
Joseph McRae Mellichamp

First published in Great Britain in 2024

SPCK
SPCK Group
Studio 101
The Record Hall
16–16A Baldwin's Gardens
London EC1N 7RJ

www.spck.org.uk

British Library Cataloguing-in-Publication Data
A catalogue record for this book is available from the British Library

ISBN 978–0–281–08926–0
eBook ISBN 978–0–281–08927–7

1 3 5 7 9 10 8 6 4 2

Typeset by Manila Typesetting Company
First printed in Great Britain by Clays Ltd

eBook by Manila Typesetting Company

Produced on paper from sustainable sources

John C. Lennox MA PhD DPhil DSc FISSR is Emeritus Professor of Mathematics at the University of Oxford and Emeritus Fellow in Mathematics and the Philosophy of Science at Green Templeton College. He is also a Fellow of the International Society for Science and Religion on which topic he has lectured at many prestigious institutions around the world. He has publicly debated Richard Dawkins and Christopher Hitchens, among others. He is also the author of many books including *Cosmic Chemistry: Do God and science mix?*; *Can Science Explain Everything?*; *Against the Flow: The inspiration of Daniel in an age of relativism* and *God and Stephen Hawking: Whose design is it anyway?*

Joseph McRae Mellichamp is Emeritus Professor of Management Science at the University of Alabama. In addition to academic research, he has published study guides for several important books, including *Mere Christianity, The Man in the Mirror* and *The Training of the Twelve*. He and his wife Peggy have spoken at more than 150 universities and colleges and made more than 35 international ministry trips in their work with the Faculty Ministry of CRU, which they helped to set up in the 1970s and 1980s.

Contents

Part 3

GENESIS 16.1—19.38

Part 4

GENESIS 20.1—22.19

Part 5

GENESIS 22.20—25.11

Foreword

We human beings are unique in that we are the only members of God's creation to be created in his image. One wonderful aspect of that image is that we are persons with the capacity to make friends, not only[1] with our fellow human beings but also with God himself.

Only two people in Scripture are individually named as friends of God. Three times over, Scripture tells us that Abraham was such a person. In Chronicles, King Jehoshaphat says in a prayer: 'Did you not, our God, drive out the inhabitants of this land before your people Israel, and give it forever to the descendants of Abraham your friend?' (2 Chron. 20.7). Isaiah the prophet later encourages the people not to fear with a word from God acknowledging Abraham as his friend: 'But you, Israel, my servant, Jacob, whom I have chosen, the offspring of Abraham, my friend' (Isa. 41.8). Finally, the apostle James records that Abraham demonstrated by his behaviour that his faith in God was real: '"Abraham believed God, and it was counted to him as righteousness" – and he was called a friend of God' (Jas. 2.23).

But what does it mean to be a friend of God? And how is it possible to become one? It is one thing to talk about friendship with God; it is entirely another thing to experience it. This study guide is designed to show you that, by learning to trust God like Abraham did, you too can become a friend of God through the Lord Jesus Christ who laid down his life and rose again in order to make it happen:

> Greater love has no one than this, that someone lay down his life for his friends. You are my friends if you do what I command you. No longer do I call you servants, for the servant does not know what his master is doing; but I have called you friends, for all that I have heard from my Father I have made known to you.
> (John 15.13–15)

Enjoy the journey.

* * *

I am deeply grateful to my friend Rae Mellichamp for writing this study guide to my book *Friend of God: The inspiration of Abraham in an age of doubt*. On the basis of his experience running study groups on Daniel, he has already done sterling work in producing an excellent guide to accompany my earlier book *Against the Flow: The inspiration of Daniel in an age of relativism*.

John C. Lennox

How to use this guide

This study guide has two essential aims:

1. Each chapter opens with a section that summarizes the relevant chapter in John Lennox's book *Friend of God*. It is assumed that the reader has already read the whole chapter in that book, and the purpose of the summary is to help refresh and reinforce the memory as well as to provide pointers for personal reflection or group discussion along the way.
2. There then follows a series of 'application questions' that are designed to get the reader thinking about the ways in which Abraham's life serves as a model for faithful living today. What have we learned about Abraham, as well as Sarah, Lot and the other characters in Abraham's story, that we can absorb and apply in our own lives, as we seek to be faithful friends of God in a world of widespread doubt and disbelief?

The authors hope that readers will find both the summaries and the application questions helpful as they work through the book, while recognizing that some may prefer to go straight to the application questions after having read the relevant chapter in *Friend of God*.

Whichever way you choose to use this guide, may God bless you in your studies!

INTRODUCTION

1
Why Abraham matters

The biblical account of Abraham's life and significance could well be framed as a tale of two cities.

- The account starts in the Old Testament with the Genesis record of the building of two cities. The first is Babel or Babylon.
- In the New Testament, Abraham is described as a man who was looking for the second city whose designer and builder is God.

That city appears in the book of Revelation as the New Jerusalem and is contrasted with Babylon the Great. Thus, the entire Bible can be thought of as a tale of two cities.

As we will soon see, Abraham is one of the most outstanding and influential individuals in world history. Professor Lennox has previously written about two other well-known biblical characters:

- Joseph, who administered the economy of Egypt;
- Daniel, who led the administrations of Babylon and its successor Medo-Persia.

In terms of influence, neither Joseph nor Daniel compares with their common ancestor Abraham.

Though he had no political or administrative role,

- more than half the world's population regard him as their spiritual father;
- the Jews and Muslims claim him as their physical progenitor.

In terms of references in the New Testament,

- Joseph is mentioned six times;
- Daniel is mentioned once;
- Abraham is mentioned more than 60 times.

Abraham figures significantly in the books of Romans, Galatians and Hebrews.

- In these letters he is given as an example of great faith.
- Particularly we read of his migration from Mesopotamia to Canaan and the inheritance of his offspring of the land.

Abraham's experience is opposite to those of Joseph and Daniel.

- Abraham was called to leave Babylon, to which Daniel would be deported and which he would eventually administer.
- Abraham was forcibly ejected from Egypt, to which Joseph would be sent as a captive and which he would ultimately administer.

Abraham never wielded administrative power.

- He lived with relatives in Ur (Babylonia).
- He moved to Haran in northern Mesopotamia.
- He migrated west and lived a nomadic life as head of a small clan in Canaan.

God called Abraham

- to be the genetic ancestor of a nation;
- to be the one through whom he would bless the world.

Joseph and Daniel are examples of this.

Who was Abraham?

- He was no superhuman super-hero.
- He was a flawed man.

Abraham's wife Sarah was involved in these events.

- She was old and childless.
- She proposed that he take her Egyptian servant Hagar as a surrogate wife to fulfil God's promise of an heir.
- Hagar and her son Ishmael were expelled upon the birth of Abraham and Sarah's son, Isaac.

God certainly used the struggles of Abraham and Sarah to fulfil his purposes.

Trust was a key issue in Abraham and Sarah's relationship and it is key throughout the Bible.

- Faith/trust is evidence-based, not superficial credulity.
- It is a trust that God will put to the test.

For Abraham's descendants to be a blessing to the world, Isaac needed to have descendants of his own.

- The story of how Isaac's wife was found is riveting.
- The Bible relates how Isaac's spiritual descendants have blessed the world.
- And one of his descendants, Jesus the Messiah, is central.

In a discussion recorded in John 8,

- Jesus claims: 'Truly, truly, I say to you, before Abraham was, I am';
- the Jews had said they were Abraham's offspring;
- Jesus responds: 'I know that you are offspring of Abraham; yet you seek to kill me . . . If you were Abraham's children, you would be doing the works Abraham did.'

To summarize: though the Jews were descended from Abraham,

- Jesus did not count them as Abraham's children, because they didn't share his attitude to God.

Thus, in a spiritual sense, a person can be counted as a child of Abraham without being physically descended from him. The essential criterion is faith in God.

In Matthew 3, John the Baptist had encountered similar misunderstandings.

- When John saw the Pharisees and Sadducees coming to him, he said that God could raise up children for Abraham from the stones.
- John was warning them not to rely on their lineage.

In Romans 4, Paul explains justification by faith.

- Faith was counted to Abraham as righteousness.
- This was before he was circumcised. (Circumcision was a sign of his faith.)

And the result: 'For in Christ Jesus you are all sons of God, through faith' (Galatians 3.26).

Thus, if we are Christ's through faith in him, we are also Abraham's offspring and his heirs.

- Being an heir is a legal status relating to inheritance.
- God made a legal commitment to Abraham 4,000 years ago, which is still in force.

This can be seen in the examples of four of Abraham's offspring:

- Ishmael and Isaac;
- Esau and Jacob.

Through Isaac and Jacob, God was choosing a line of inheritance based on faith, not genealogy.

One of our main objectives in this study will be to understand inheritance from God's perspective.

Application questions

1 We begin our study by considering the importance of Abraham in biblical history. Why do you suppose it is that Abraham isn't always given the attention and respect he is due in this regard?
2 We see in Scripture that God intended to bless the world through the descendants of Abraham. A startling piece of evidence that confirms this assertion is that 20% of Nobel prizes have been awarded to Jewish people, even though they constitute less than a tenth of 1% the world population! Can you think of some other ways we have been blessed by the people of Abraham?
3 In some respects, Abraham's story focuses on descendants. And, for believers, Abraham's most significant descendant is the Lord Jesus Christ. His life, death on the cross and resurrection make it possible for us to become sons and daughters of God and to have eternal life with him. Do you consider yourself to be related to Abraham through your faith in Jesus? Can you explain how?
4 What is the essential element in the transaction between God and Abraham?

2
Abraham – a historical figure?

Saying that Abraham was a historical figure assumes that

- he really did exist as an actual person;
- he lived at a particular time and place.

It has become fashionable in recent times to question the historicity of events and persons in both the Old and New Testaments. But manuscript and archaeological evidence is strong. The following are examples of research that supports the accuracy of the Bible:

- *The Book of Acts in the Setting of Hellenistic History* by Colin Hemer[2]
- *Can We Trust the Gospels?* by Peter J. Williams.[3]

Here is one example of how difficult this process can be:

- Genesis describes a treaty Abraham made with the king of Gerar. If a copy of the treaty were found, that would enhance the credibility of the Genesis account. It has not been found.
- In order to find it, archaeologists would have to unearth the royal palace and locate the archive room.
- Assuming the archive room could be found, would the archives be there? That depends on the material used.
- The treaty might have been made orally, in which case no record could be recovered.
- And there is one further reason why no copy has ever been found. The site of Gerar has never been identified!

On these grounds, Alan Millard writes in *Treasures from Bible Times* that

- it is most unlikely any record will be found of Abraham or Joseph in Egypt;
- the biblical narrative is very much in keeping with the era in question.[4]

Kenneth Kitchen suggests in *On the Reliability of the Old Testament* that there are five kinds of biblical narrative texts:

- royal historical texts
- autobiographical and biographical texts
- historical legends
- purely fictional tales, excluding historical people
- tales of mythology.[5]

Kitchen places the Abraham narrative in the second category and argues that the fairest assessment based on the biblical narrative is as follows:

- a real historical family of a man named Terah existed around 2,000 BC in and around Ur;
- the family moved northwestwards and Abraham's family moved into Canaan;
- his grandson, Joseph, cared for the family in Egypt;
- Abraham passed on family lore to his son Isaac.

This view is supported by R. K. Harrison in his *Introduction to the Old Testament.*[6]

More detailed material may be found in *Essays on the Patriarchal Narratives,* edited by A. R. Millard and D. J. Wiseman.[7]

The New Testament supports the historicity of Abraham.

- Abraham is included in the genealogies of Jesus in Matthew and Luke.
- Jesus clearly regarded Abraham as a historical figure (John 8.56–58).

The minimalist character of Hebrew narrative is partly responsible for unanswered questions.

- It captures the protagonist only at critical points in his or her life.
- It focuses on actions rather than moods, emotions and thoughts.

The importance of Abraham's story to Genesis is underscored by the fact that it occupies one third of the book.

Application questions

1. Have you heard anyone lately questioning biblical characters, events, places, times or history? Were their questions based on solid manuscript and archaeological evidence?
2. After reading the text, what do you think is the challenge facing archaeologists who are trying to verify biblical history?
3. The assessment by Kenneth Kitchen is impressive. He claims that the truth of Abraham's family background and movements is backed up as they are revealed in an autobiographical text. Is this good evidence or likely to be criticized?
4. The story of Abraham occupies one third of the book of Genesis. What does this say about the importance of this man to the biblical narrative?

3

Structure and thought flow in the book of Genesis

We will now survey the structure of Genesis as a whole. The book of Genesis uses phrases called *toledoths*:

- 'This is the account of . . .'
- 'These are the generations of . . .'

Here is the organization of Genesis:

The beginning

1. The creation of the universe and human beings (1.1—2.3).
2. What it is to be human and the beginning of sin (2.4—4.26). The generations of the heavens and the earth (2.4).
3. From Adam to the judgement of the world (5.1—9.29). The generations of Adam (5.1—6.8); Noah (6.9—9.29).

The new beginning

4. Abraham and his sons (10.1—25.11). The generations of Noah, Shem, Terah; the death of Abraham.
5. Isaac and his sons (25.12—35.29). The generations of Ishmael (25.12), Isaac (25.19); the death of Isaac.
6. Jacob and his sons (36.1—50.26). The generations of Esau (36.1), Jacob (37.2); the deaths of Jacob and Esau.

We can see from this that God's choice of the line of inheritance is indicated by various literary devices.

- The lesser lines are given a brief description followed by the *toledoth* and the main line.

A summary of the major sections of Genesis.

Section 1

- The nature of God, the status of the universe and the status of human beings.
- God created the universe by his word, and human beings are uniquely made in God's image.
- This section is a powerful assault on the naturalism of the ancient and modern worlds.

Section 2

- The basic parameters of human existence. We are made from dust, have an aesthetic sense, need food, are curious, work and have relationships with family and others.
- Life at its highest entails a relationship with God defined by his word, which is the essence of morality in freedom and responsibility.
- Human sin breaks the relationship and infects the world. Yet God makes provision and promises that one day humanity will triumph.
- This section traces morality back to its defining source in God and constitutes an assault on the dominant moral philosophy of the present Western world: utilitarianism.
- This philosophy, a consequentialist view of morality, suggests that an action is to be judged solely in terms of its consequences on the principle of the maximum benefit for the maximum number of people.
- If actions are not subjugated by conformity to a higher sense of right and wrong, these can lead to undesirable results: genocide, for example.

Section 3

- The development of the human race from Adam, and its increasingly violent and corrupt behaviour.
- In Section 1, God's word separates earth from sea, and in Section 3, God brings judgement on the world.

- The New Testament in Matthew 24.37 uses the Flood narrative to show how the past foreshadowed the future. 'As were the days of Noah, so will be [the future].'

The first three sections of Genesis lay the foundation for three major biblical doctrines:

- creation
- sin and the promise of redemption
- judgement and salvation.

Each of the first three sections includes a reference to the creation of humans, thus we have three different aspects of the uniqueness of humans as God's image bearers.

The second half of Genesis represents a new beginning for humanity after the Flood.

- In Section 4 the narrative concentrates on a particular person, Abraham, and his sons.
- In Section 5 the narrative focuses on Isaac and his sons.
- In Section 6 the narrative focuses on Jacob and his sons, particularly Joseph.

'I am the God of Abraham, and the God of Isaac, and the God of Jacob' summarizes the second half of Genesis.

Some conclusions:

- Leon Kass, in *The Beginning of Wisdom*, says that the biblical narratives present human life in all its moral ambiguity.[8]
- They present not simply what happened in a particular time and place but show what always happens.
- They are a mirror in which the complexity of our own lives is reflected.

Genesis shows us what is first in importance when it comes to understanding fundamental things: God, the universe, life, language, morality, relationships, sin, death, salvation and much more.

The order in which these things are communicated is important.

- The narrative begins not with the moral failure of humans, but with their value as made in God's image.
- It continues by relating the devastation that results from misuse of God-given capacities.

God begins anew after the Flood.

- He calls Abram to leave his own country, to start again in a new land to live God's way.
- We learn about the complexities of this path back to God through the lives of flawed men and women – the patriarchs, their wives and families.

Here is a summary of the stages in the life of Abraham.

Background (10.1—11.32)
- Gentile nations descended from Noah: Nimrod
- The city and tower of Babel: making a name
- The death of Terah

Stage 1 (12.1—15.21)
- God's call to Abram
- Abram's denial of his wife among Egyptians
- The promise of name, seed and inheritance
- Justification by faith

Stage 2 (16.1—19.38)
- Trust in God's promise or the works of the flesh?
- A substitute wife: Ishmael born to Hagar
- Lot: his daughters and his seed

Stage 3 (20.1—22.24)

- Security in God or in his gift?
- Abraham's denial of his wife among Philistines
- Isaac born and Ishmael cast out
- The offering of Isaac
- Justification by works

Stage 4 (23.1—25.11)

- Sarah's death and burial
- A wife for Isaac from the Gentiles
- Abraham's death and burial

Application questions

1. The Hebrew word for generations or descendants, *toledoth*, is used to mark off distinct sections in the book of Genesis. The prominent occurrences are: 'This is the account of . . .' and 'These are the generations of . . .' Do you think that knowing this makes understanding the structure of the book less of a challenge?
2. Do you see that the *toledoths* under the heading of 'The new beginning' ('Abraham and his sons' and 'Isaac and his sons') clearly alert us to what is coming? We've left one out – what is it?
3. Here is a wonderful statement: 'Life at its highest entails a relationship with God defined by his word, which is the essence of morality in freedom and responsibility.' Would you subscribe to that? Can you conceive of any other definition of life at its highest?
4. The New Testament in Matthew 24.37 and Luke 17.26 uses the Flood narrative to show how the past foreshadows the future: 'As were the days of Noah so will be . . .' In what ways are our days already like the days of Noah?
5. The phrase 'I am the God of Abraham, and the God of Isaac, and the God of Jacob' summarizes the second half of Genesis. Explain how this is so.

6 'The stages in the life of Abraham' is a very useful way of framing the Genesis narrative. Just consider the first entry in each of the first three stages: 'God's call to Abram', 'Trust in God's promise or the works of the flesh?' and 'Security in God or in his gift?' What is the connection between these stage elements and life at its highest?

Part I

GENESIS 10.1—11.32

1

The city that reached for the sky

Genesis 10 and 11 give important background information to the Mesopotamian culture from which Abraham came.

- The Table of Nations describes the repopulation of the earth after the Flood.
- The patriarchal tradition was probably passed down in Egypt.
- Mesopotamian culture flourished from the third millennium BC.

Genesis 11 concentrates on the construction of one particular city: Babel (Babylon).

- A new beginning: 'The beginning of his kingdom . . .' (Gen. 10.10).

The last occurrence of God's speech in Genesis 1, 'God said to them', gives insight into what it means to be made in the image of God. It means that

- we can hear and understand what God says;
- we can respond to what God says.

Two construction projects contrasted.

A divine construction project
- God creates the universe by speaking his word.
- Humans are made in God's image from the earth.

A human construction project
- Initiated by humans speaking their words.
- They use bricks of clay from the earth.

God's construction was alive, theirs lifeless.
This results in two outcomes:

- A world for the habitation of humans to enjoy fellowship with God.
- A world for the glorification of self: 'Let us make a name for ourselves.'

Aristotle said:

> Nature . . . has endowed man alone with the power of speech . . . Speech . . . serves to indicate what is useful and what is harmful, and . . . what is just and what is unjust. It is the sharing of a common view on these matters that makes a household and a state[9].

- The household is the partnership constituted for the needs of daily life.
- The union of several households for the sake of non-daily needs is the village.
- The union of several villages for the sake of self-sufficiency is the city.

Two fundamental questions that help us to understand what was at stake here are:

- What is something made *of* (Aristotle's material cause)? The foundation of Babel was clay bricks.
- What is something made *for* (Aristotle's final cause)? Babel was made for reputation.

'Making a name' by building a city and tower in order to avoid dispersion was an affront to God, who had made humans and commanded them to multiply and fill the earth.

- God promised Abraham in Genesis 12.2, 'I will . . . make your name great.'
- All nations of the earth have been blessed by Abraham and his reputation.

Secularization occurs when people turn their attention from worlds beyond towards this world and this time.

- Jacques Ellul says that the city represents humanity's attempt to replace God.[10]

In the secular city, the tower is a symbol for humanity as the creator of its own meaning. Philip Nobel, writing for the American Enterprise Institute, suggests:

- 'The most primal motivation for skyscraper construction is to stake a claim'.
- 'Skyscrapers are built to make space, they are built to make money, but they are also built to make a point: they are built to awe.'[11]

The ideology of the modern skyscraper is essentially that of ancient Babel:

- pushing out the boundaries, exceeding the limits, flaunting wealth and power;
- reaching for the sky and grasping at immortality.

The tower, or ziggurat, in Babylon was called *Etemenanki*: 'the house of the foundation of heaven and earth'.

- It had a temple at the top where the gods could come down to humans.
- The builders probably thought that, the bigger the tower, the more powerful the gods who would come.

God made a chilling remark about the builders of Babel in Genesis 11.5–7:

- nothing they proposed to do would be impossible to them;
- however, some of their projects would prove disastrous.

God clearly regarded the Babel project as directed against him.

- It was a massive glorification of human ego and prowess in rebellion against God.
- Rebellion against God runs throughout the biblical narrative and will be destroyed only by the return of Jesus.

C. S. Lewis's novel *That Hideous Strength*[12] shows the dangers of using morally unbridled science and technology to try to alter and control humankind.

Another event in history marked a reversal of what happened at Babel: the creation of the Church on the Day of Pentecost.

- On that day, people were suddenly empowered to understand in their language what the apostles were saying about the mighty work of God.
- It connected linguistic commonality with the Holy Spirit. Holiness was the opposite of what Babel stood for.

Pentecost involved God coming down to dwell on earth.

The story of Babel provides an explanation for what is happening in many countries today and for the fractured society we now inhabit. Jonathan Haidt writes in *The Atlantic*:

- 'We are cut off from one another and the past.'[13]
- Social media has weakened factors necessary for democracy by spreading dislike, distrust, outrage and hate.

There are many kinds of 'language' that fragment our culture.

- The old don't understand the young and vice versa.
- There are languages of political correctness and incorrectness.

Old-style healthy and true tolerance ('I disagree with you, but will defend your right to say it') has been replaced by a relativistic paralysis of criticism:

- I dare not offend, or the thought police will act.

Jesus refused to get involved in controversies, and Paul warned us to avoid them (Titus 3.9).

- They did not go around looking for trouble.
- Nor did they placate the opposition.

Russell Moore says, 'We need a shared story, but a story without tension is no story at all.' In our story, Moore, says, God

- 'brought us [Israel] out of the land and slavery of Egypt';
- '"raised Jesus from the dead"'.[14]

God called us to unity.

- We don't find it by developing better technology to rebuild the tower. Sometimes God frustrates what we are doing because it is killing us.
- The kind of unity we need is what is right and pleasing in the sight of God.

There are legendary accounts in later Jewish and Islamic literature of confrontation between Abraham and Nimrod.

- Nimrod persecuted Abraham.
- Nimrod intended to kill Abraham, but he left for Canaan.
- Nimrod was slain by Esau, who was jealous of his hunting skill.

A common element in these legends is that Abraham was a monotheist and a protester against idolatry.

For our purposes, the main contrast between Nimrod and Abraham is in the way we make our name.

- How do we find significance?
- Where do we get answers to big questions?

In his best-selling book, *Homo Deus*,[15] Yuval Noah Harari presents a grandiose transhumanist agenda to

- abolish physical death by technical means;
- enhance human happiness by changing biochemistry;
- upgrade humans into gods – Homo Sapiens to Homo Deus.

This reminds us of *That Hideous Strength* by C. S. Lewis, which gives a vision of human life that is independent of biology.[16]

Application questions

1. God's construction project resulted in a world for the habitation of humans with the possibility of enjoying fellowship with God. Humanity's construction project resulted in a world for the glorification of self. We are told that God's project was alive; theirs was lifeless. Can you explain how this is true?
2. In constructing the city of Babel, we learn that God was dispensed with altogether. How did this happen? Did Nimrod and his associates plan a city in which God was intentionally left out? Why? Are there modern-day parallels you can identify?
3. Community is certainly an important aspect of life. But regarding community as more important than fulfilling God's specific purposes for our lives is not wise. However, people do this every day. Can you give some examples?
4. Secularization occurs when people turn their attention from worlds beyond towards this world and this time. Is this happening at all today? Give some examples. Is this a problem for you?
5. Professor Lennox observes that, in the secular city, the tower is a symbol for humanity as the creator of its own meaning. In what ways do you create your identity and meaning? Are you building any towers?
6. We learn that the Day of Pentecost and the creation of the Church marked a reversal of what happened at Babel. Can you explain this? Had you ever thought of it before?
7. Social media has weakened factors that are necessary to sustain democracies. These include: social networks with high levels of trust, strong institutions and shared stories. Could you describe how these factors feature in your own experience and have you seen any impact upon them from social media in your lifetime?
8. The main contrast between Abraham and Nimrod is in the way they chose to make their names. Abraham did so by obedience to God in leaving his home and moving to the land of Canaan and following God throughout his life. Nimrod tried to make a name for himself by building cities and towers. How do we assess the name each of these men ultimately ended up with? What do you think?

2

From Shem to Abram

Ur and its idolatry

The detailed description of Babel in Genesis might lead us to expect that Abram was a native. Not so.

- Abram was a native of Ur, which dates from 3800 BC and was the capital of lower Mesopotamia, located in southern Iraq.
- Abram's life dates are difficult to establish (Kenneth Kitchen places Abram's life at approximately 2000–1900 BC[17]).
- One of the pieces of evidence relevant to the dating of Abraham is his battle with a coalition of Eastern kings, which is reported in Genesis 14.
- After its fall, circa 2000, Mesopotamia was divided between a series of kingdoms. Thus, from about 2000 to 1750 we have a period during which power alliances were common in the region.

Although the whole country worshipped a common high-level pantheon, each city-state had its own patron deity.

- The deity of Ur was Nanna, the Sumerian moon-god of time (lunar months).
- The name of the city, Ur, is derived from the god's name – 'the abode (UNUG) of Nanna'.
- The crescent moon was used as a symbol of this god and later adopted as the symbol of Islam.

Genesis 1 constitutes a protest against such idolatry by identifying the sun and moon as lights, not deities.

Ur was a centre of trade and commerce.

- It had an advanced culture and impressive architecture.
- Its central edifice was a three-storeyed ziggurat built of sun-dried bricks and topped by a shrine to the god Nanna.

Excavation of the Royal Cemetery at Ur uncovered:

- treasures of gold, silver, bronze and semi-precious stones;
- evidence that kings were buried with court officials;
- musical instruments, golden weapons and more.

All this provides evidence of an advanced civilization.

Mesopotamian education was mostly for boys from wealthy homes and consisted of:

- writing (cuneiform – wedge-shaped marks on clay)
- history and mathematics
- geography, zoology, botany, astronomy, engineering, medicine and architecture.

Abram and Sumerian idolatry

Joshua 24.2–3 implies that Abram's immediate ancestors were not committed to the one true God (v. 2).

- Abram was 60 years old when Noah died.
- He was 110 when Shem died.

It is said that Noah walked faithfully with God (Genesis 6.9), although his positive influence waned in later life.

Information about Abram's contact with Noah may have appeared in the book of Jashar, which is referenced in Joshua 10.12–13 and 2 Samuel 1.17–18. A medieval Midrash text of this name tells us that

- Abram was 10 years old when his brother fathered Sarai.
- Abram learned the instruction of Elohim from Noah.

G. Roux, in his book *Ancient Iraq*, suggests that religion held such a prominent position in Mesopotamian society because their society felt utterly dependent on the will of the gods.[18]

It has been suggested that multiple connections existed between idol worship and Abram's family.

- His wife Sarai's name is related to the moon-god Sin.
- His niece Milcah's name may be derived from 'daughter of Sin'.
- Jewish legends say that Abram's father, Terah, was an idol-maker.

Worship of 'other gods' is the number one offence against the one true God – it heads the list of the Ten Commandments (see Exod. 20.1–6).

There are two ways of looking at idols:

- their physical appearance – statues, figurines, icons;
- what they represent – they symbolize power.

In the West, the dominant worldview of naturalism,

- with confidence in the power of the human mind,
- and its attribution of creative powers to nature,

is as idolatrous as the philosophies of the ancient Near East. The secular pressure to trust almost anything other than God is everywhere.

The effect of the sexual revolution is that many young people trust sexual relationships to give them the meaning and identity they long for.

- This is idolatry.
- It often turns into self-destructive desires.

The message of Abraham is that fulfilment cannot be found in idols, but only in a relationship with God.

Idolatry is an expression of the same proud rebellion against God that began in Genesis and involved three fundamental human desires:

- an appetite for food;
- a desire for aesthetic satisfaction;
- a longing for human flourishing.

God permitted the first humans to eat of all the trees around them in the garden except for one.

- God gave them dignity as moral beings.
- They had the capacity to say yes or no to what God said.
- They could either trust the Creator and obey his word, or assert their independence from him.

They were persuaded that, if they wished to be truly free, they should ignore God's restrictive condition, follow their instinctive desires and eat the fruit.

From the beginning, God wanted humans to gain knowledge.

- He instructed them to explore the garden.
- He asked them to name the animals.

Instead, they gained the knowledge of good and evil. Many people today believe that God is against human flourishing and wishes to spoil their enjoyment of what life has to offer.

The question of whether or not to trust and obey God's word is the central issue of the book of Genesis, and indeed of life itself. It is the most fundamental of life's battles – whether to put our faith in God or to put it in something or someone else, which would be idolatry.

Application questions

1 You have probably read the city name Ur in Babylonia many times without really giving it much thought. Here we learn that it was

the capital city of lower Mesopotamia. It was a centre of trade and culture, with impressive architecture. Does knowing this change your view of God calling Abram to leave his home?

2 The citizens of Ur were given over to the worship of idols. We normally think of someone leaving their home and relatives as a bad thing! Why do you think it might have been a good thing for God to call Abram away from Ur?
3 Noting that worship of idols is the subject of the very first of the Ten Commandments can give us an idea of how important it is to God and why we ought to avoid it at all costs. How are you doing in this area? Do you have any idols? They are unlikely to be statues and icons, but could be aspirations or other things that have captured your attention and taken it away from God.
4 The message of Abram is that true fulfilment cannot be found in idols, physical or otherwise, but only in a relationship with God. Is this a message people today need to hear? How can we communicate it?
5 'The question of whether or not to trust and obey God's word is the central issue of the book of Genesis, and indeed of life itself. It is the most fundamental of life's battles – whether to put our faith in God or to put it in something or someone else, which would be idolatry.' How are you faring in this battle?

Part 2

GENESIS 12.1—15.21

3

The call of Abram

God's call and promise (Gen. 12.1–20)

God calls Abram to journey to another land and promises that he will become a great nation and bless the world.

From Ur to Haran

- The reason for the journey is explained by Stephen: 'After his father died, God removed [Abram] from there into this land' (Acts 7.4).
- The city of Haran, like Ur, was devoted to moon (idol) worship.
- Was Terah grieving the earlier loss of his son, Haran, who died in Ur?
- Had Abram convinced Terah of the existence of the one true God?

The God who speaks

Abram's first major discovery was that there is a God who speaks.

- God said he would do these things for Abram:
  - show him a land;
  - make of him a great nation;
  - bless him and make his name great;
  - make him a blessing;
  - bless those who bless him;
  - curse those who dishonour him;
  - bless all the families of the earth through him.

- God's promise to make Abram's name great recalls the motivation for those who built the city of Babel.

The first and most important 'foundation' Abram sought is faith in God, not in ourselves.

Dialogue between God and humans is central to biblical revelation.

- A lifelong dialogue started between God and Abram.
- Scientific colleagues might object: 'You don't believe Abraham actually heard God's voice?'

So we are left with a choice:

- the call to Abram was either a 'voice in his head'; or
- there is a Creator God who communicates.

The Bible claims to be the word of God in written form; Jesus is the Word of God in human form.

- Abram is not the only person to whom God spoke.
- The prophets proclaimed what God said to them.
- Those who heard Jesus were hearing God speak (John 14.8–11; 16.12–15).

One reason for believing that God spoke to Abram is the conviction that Jesus is the Son of God.

- This conviction is rational and based on objective and experiential evidence.
- Science cannot adjudicate the existence of either God or his voice. It is limited to investigating natural phenomena.
- Many contemporary claims that God spoke to someone are spurious, so caution needs to be exercised here.

There is no scientific reason to deny, and many rational reasons to affirm, that God has spoken to individuals.

- He spoke audibly to Jesus on three occasions.
- He spoke to the prophets and apostles.
- He spoke to Abram to communicate his promise.

The voice to Abram said in Hebrew, *Lech lecha* (literally 'Get yourself going'). This can be understood as:

- an internal odyssey to the roots of your soul;
- a call to separate from the past and journey with God.

The late Chief Rabbi Lord Jonathan Sacks wrote, 'These words are the most consequential in the history of mankind.'[19]

He further stated, '*Lech lecha* means: Leave behind you all that makes human beings predictable, unfree, able to blame others and evade responsibility.' It means to challenge the idols of the age.

Jesus' call to his disciples is just as radical as God's call to Abraham.

- He insists that our commitment to him be unequivocal.
- He insists that we deny ourselves and follow him.

Jesus expects radical commitment, but he does not expect it to be a completely irrational leap of faith (2 Pet. 1.3).

Application questions

1. The journey from Ur to Canaan, with a stopover in Haran, raises some interesting questions. One question is: what was the reason for the delay in Haran, aside from the fact that Abram had relatives there? Luke refers us to Stephen's defence in the New Testament, in which he states, 'After his father died, God removed [Abram] from there into this land' (Acts 7:4). What do you think?
2. Abram's first discovery, we are told, was that there is a God who speaks. He instructed him to leave Mesopotamia and he promised him gifts and blessings. These promises are central to Genesis and the

Bible. That there is a God who speaks is truly remarkable. Have you heard God speak? If so, how?

3 The scientific implications of there being a God who speaks are astounding. We have a choice to make: either the call of Abraham was an auditory hallucination or there is a Creator God who speaks. If there is a Creator God who speaks, then the purely materialistic view of the universe is false – it is not a closed system of cause and effect. Explain why this is monumental.

4 The command *lech lecha* is full of meaning. It suggests an internal odyssey to the roots of one's soul and a call to separate from the past and journey with God. This is a radical way of apprehending what our life's journey should be. These words may be the most consequential in the history of humankind! Have you experienced such a call?

4
From Haran to Canaan

Abram's possessions were many. Some think that they were mentioned before the people to indicate the value priority in Abram's mind at the time: possessions first, then people.

There are elements of ambiguity, hesitancy, even uncertainty here in which Abram's humanity is evident as he matured in his understanding of God's call. And the same will be true of us.

One of the great lessons for us to grasp from Abram's story is that we can be involved in the great project he started – involved as God's spiritual children, travelling on the greatest journey of all.

- Leon Kass suggests that Abram obeyed the voice because he was an ambitious man who wished to have a great name and power.
- Could it not be something more: an inner longing to find a greater narrative in which to frame his life?

Our response to God's call is a complex mixture of God's voice and our desires.

It seems as if Genesis sets the promise to Abram to make his name great against the background of Babylon's attempt to do the same in order to differentiate between two ways of living:

- Babylon's way, or
- Abram's way.

The difference between these two ways of living is what the biblical narrative is all about.

Leaving has already been discussed in Genesis: at the beginning of the book it is said that marriage involves human beings leaving their parents and cleaving to their husband or wife.

Now Abram is called to leave

- his family
- his culture and native land.

One way of thinking of Abram's spiritual journey is in terms of 'tests' he underwent. Kass mentions eleven:

- Abram called to leave his home: the promise of seed;
- Sarai in trouble in Egypt;
- Abram in dispute with Lot;
- Lot in trouble – Abram rescues him;
- trouble between Hagar and Sarah;
- Abram and the covenant of circumcision;
- Abram hosts three strangers;
- Lot and Sodom in trouble;
- Sarah in trouble in Gerar;
- trouble with Ishmael;
- Abraham called to sacrifice Isaac, the promised seed.[20]

Abram's journey, like all human journeys, has multiple facets: moral, spiritual, intellectual and geographical.

Chief Rabbi Jonathan Sacks wrote: 'All other civilisations rise and fall. The faith of Abraham survives.'

Monotheism is not a linear development from polytheism. Jonathan Sacks continued: 'Monotheism, by discovering the transcendental God . . . who stands outside the universe and creates it, made it possible . . . to believe that life has a meaning, not just a mythic or scientific explanation.'[21]

God, the source of all ultimate meaning, called to Abram. It was the first great 'Follow me' call in history. We may wonder what led up to it.

- Were there years of questioning whether something existed besides nature?
- Were there increasing doubts about the rationality of worshipping the moon?

Maybe Abram had seen through the polytheism of the day.

Another important piece of information about Abram's call is found in the book of Acts. It highlights a similarity and a contrast between Abram and Paul.

- Both Abram and Paul saw the glory of God; both were sent on journeys, but in opposite directions.
- Abram was called out of the Gentile world, whereas Paul was sent back to the Gentiles as a missionary ambassador.

Paul's gospel outreach to the Gentile world was a major fulfilment of God's promise to Abram to bring blessing to the world.

Arrival in the land

When Abram and his company came to the land of Canaan, they passed through the land until they arrived at Shechem.

- There God promised, 'To your offspring I will give this land.'
- Then Abram built an altar to the Lord and journeyed on.

The 700 km journey from Haran to Shechem lacks any detailed comments.

- The land was occupied by Canaanites, descendants of Noah's grandson Canaan.
- Canaanites were earth worshipping, fertility obsessed and licentious.

Throughout history, land has been an extremely important commodity. This was particularly true of the ancient Near East.

- This land grant was no mere smallholding.
- It was enough land to support a family and a nation!

To no other individual has God promised land in this way. Abraham is unique in history.

- God gave him this land for a nation.
- From this nation the Messiah would come – the human line of God-become-flesh, Jesus Christ.

Interestingly, God gave Abraham no inheritance in the land during his lifetime.

- The Feast of the Passover is regarded as the beginning of Israel.
- Joshua led the Israelites into the land to settle it 40 years after the Passover.

But this is not the end of the story. The promised land has been the subject of violent wars and disputes between those who claim to be Abraham's descendants: Jews, Christians and Muslims.

This might lead us to ask: why did it all turn out this way? The writer of Hebrews suggests that the Jews were focused on a heavenly country and city: 'These all died in faith, not having received the things promised' (see Heb. 11.13–16, 39–40).

Nimrod's kingdom was building cities. Abraham's was building altars. Abraham saw these altars as representative of his dealings with God; his tent-dwelling was temporary.

Genesis records the building of four altars.

- The first was at Shechem, where God appeared to Abram and made his promise.
- The second was built between Bethel and Ai (Bethel means 'house of God'; Ai means 'heap of ruins'). The concept of the house of God can denote the rule and government of God.
- The third altar was built at Mamre, where Abram settled and where subsequent patriarchs would be buried.
- The fourth altar was the one on which Abraham's son Isaac would be offered later.

Application questions

1 Some people have noted that Abram's possessions are mentioned before his companions on the journey from Haran to Canaan. They

take this as evidence that Abram cared more about possessions than people. What do you think?

2 The stay in Haran was lengthy. We can certainly understand why. Abram and his companions had family there who were established and well-off. They were probably happy to take advantage of their hospitality and not in any hurry to get back on the road. Why did they eventually leave?

3 One of the great lessons we learn from Abraham's story is that our walk with God as his children is 'the greatest journey of all'. Have you discovered this for yourself? What do you need to do to keep this truth before you as you go through life?

4 The contrast between God's promise to Abram to make his name great and the focus of Babylon to make a great name for itself is illuminating. Is our desire to create our own name and identity or is it to follow God and trust him for reputation, possessions, descendants and so on? Is it even possible to live life without thinking of these things?

5 Here is another gem that we need to understand: 'Monotheism, by discovering the transcendental God . . . who stands outside the universe and creates it, made it possible to believe . . . that life has a meaning.'[22] Could you elaborate on this? What does this have to do with the meaning of your life?

6 The contrast between Abraham and Paul is instructive. Abraham was called out of the Gentile world so he could focus on his relationship with God; Paul was called from Judaism to the Gentile world in order to explain to a predominantly Gentile audience how they could have a relationship with God. And in this, Abraham has become a blessing to the world. Has God worked in any unexpected, yet parallel, ways in your life?

5

From Canaan to Egypt

Learning what 'wife' means

Famine forced Abram to cross the frontier of the promised land and go down to Egypt. This was a risky move and he feared for his safety.

Abram put self-preservation and material prosperity above his marriage relationship.

- He rejected truth and honesty when he asked Sarai to say that she was his sister.

Abram would prosper, but God would plague Pharaoh's house until he sent Abram and Sarai away.

This is the first mention of famine in Scripture, in stark contrast to the plenty of the garden of Eden.

- It brought Abram briefly to Egypt.
- It would bring Jacob and his children to Egypt for four centuries until Moses led them back to Canaan.

What was the meaning of this famine? There is no record of

- Abram asking God;
- God telling Abram what to do.

Some people think God micromanages our lives. This episode shows that this is not so.

Parents who insist on making every decision and doing everything for their children risk leaving them

- immature;
- lacking in character.

Children need space to grow up and develop their own character and convictions. They must be allowed to make mistakes.

This is what God does for us. His guidance is in giving us moral principles that form our character.

Abram decided not to wait and starve, as he imagined he would. He left Canaan, the promised land, and went down to Egypt.

In retrospect, it may seem to have been a move in the wrong direction. It was a *lech lecha* of

- going into himself and learning about the weaknesses of his own character;
- going towards his ultimate purpose of service to his own Creator.

When we step out on our own and ultimately return, our relationship can be enhanced by the separation.

Kass describes some of the features of Egyptian culture of the time:

- it had the fertility of the Nile, technology, architecture, administration;
- it had people with the ability to manipulate certain phenomena;
- it had nature-worship: the human had no special dignity in the cosmos;
- one man, Pharaoh, believed to be a god, ruled despotically over all others.

Kass describes the Egyptians as 'rationalist technocrats'.[23]

Abram hoped to find food for his family and people in Egypt, and pasture for his flocks. He became fearful that his wife's beauty could endanger his life.

- She was no longer young but was regarded as one of the world's most beautiful women.
- She lived in a time when people may have aged less rapidly and lived longer than today.

The first words spoken by a human in the Bible were Adam's when he welcomed Eve.

- He said: 'This at last is bone of my bones and flesh of my flesh' (Gen. 2.23).
- This was followed by a biblical definition of marriage: 'Therefore a man shall leave his father and his mother and hold fast to his wife, and they shall become one flesh' (2.24).

Abram's first recorded words to Sarai are him asking her to deny her relationship with him.

- She was to say that she was his sister.
- This was actually a half-truth.

Leon Kass writes that 'a wife is not transmutable into a sister or a concubine when it suits one's purpose'.[24] True affirmation of relationships is one of life's most important lessons.

This is also a foundation of God's future city, the New Jerusalem, whose values are rooted in God's character: 'a bride adorned for her husband' (Rev. 21.2).

This is a challenge to readers who are husbands to ask themselves:

- What does 'wife' mean to me?
- How do I express that meaning?
- How have I treated my wife?
- Have I been inattentive or neglectful?
- What would she think 'wife' meant to me?

Abram seemed to have little sense that his mission in life was a joint venture with Sarai. And that also applies to some of us husbands.

Here is how Kass explains Abram's indifference towards Sarai.

- 'Rarely do great men, with great dreams, like to acknowledge their dependence.'
- 'Proud men are not given to yielding to their wives.'
- 'Before he can become a founder, and even a proper father, he must become a proper husband and appreciate Sarah as a wife.'[25]

God had promised Abram a prosperous future. Abram, for his part, decided to put his own self-preservation, well-being and material wealth above honesty, truth and the integrity of his marriage, risking prostituting his wife.

Did either of them call to God for help? We don't know.

Well-being, which could be considered the opposite of famine, has become

- a major idol of our day;
- a major subject of academic inquiry.

Christians should be at the forefront of shaping concepts of well-being. Research has found that

- there is an established correlation between a living faith in God and well-being.

And it is common in the pursuit of well-being to reject God-given norms, and to cut moral corners. This often includes setting aside marriage vows, proceeding from a destructive idolatry of the self.

Removing the God dimension from his life at this point

- left Abram at the mercy of the temptation to look after himself;
- leads us to wonder how much he understood God's commitment to him.

Jewish tradition insists that nothing indecent happened between Sarai and Pharaoh. Pharaoh discovered the truth, rebuked Abram for his dishonesty and sent him packing (Gen. 12.17–20).

This would have been profoundly embarrassing for Abram.

- We hope he was ashamed that his failure to acknowledge Sarai as his wife had increased his wealth.
- It is sad for men to have a false sense of well-being that comes from neglecting their marriage.

'Let marriage be held in honour among all . . . keep your life free from love of money' (Heb. 13.4–5).

Some lessons from this story:

- We will be embarrassed if and when we allow ourselves to be shamed by non-believers who expose our dishonesty.
- We need to avoid pretence of two kinds:
  - pretending to be what we are not;
  - pretending not to be what we are.
- We need to realize how easily we can make false assumptions about the moral convictions of others.
- We need to realize that, if God can use an Abram who really blew it, he can use us.
- We need to recognize that, in certain respects, others have higher moral standards than we do, to our shame.
- We need to be aware that all men and women are created in the image of God as moral beings. Humans are hard-wired for morality, and non-believers have a right to judge us when we fail.

Here are some observations from this episode involving Abram and Pharaoh.

- There is no indication that Pharaoh tried to recoup the wealth he showered upon Abram.
- There is speculation that Abram went to Egypt to seek out knowledge and philosophy.
- There are questions about whether Abram communicated information about God to the Egyptians.

There are a number of interesting connections between the events in Abram's journey down to Egypt and later events in Jewish history. Here are a few.

- Joseph would go down to Egypt, sold by his brothers as a slave.
- Jacob and his family would go down to live with Joseph and ultimately become slaves.
- The Egyptian woman Hagar was brought into Abram's home with the wealth they were given.

Another relationship that is sometimes marginalized or denied because of fear is our relationship with God (1 Pet. 3.13–17; 2 Cor. 11.1–4).

Paul compares loyalty to Christ with faithfulness in engagement and marriage.

Abram decided for himself to go down to Egypt, but sometimes God calls people to make that journey. For example:

- Jacob in the time of famine
- Joseph and Mary with Jesus.

Note that Scripture has some positive things to say about Egypt (e.g. Isa. 19.24–25).

Application questions

1. As Abram and his family journeyed south towards Egypt to get food for themselves and pastures for the flocks, Abram began to worry about their safety. Because Sarai was a beautiful woman, he imagined that Pharaoh may try to take her into his harem by force. Thus, Abram persuaded Sarai to tell Pharaoh she was Abram's sister. What was wrong with this ploy?
2. Some people understand Abram's excursion to Egypt as a *lech lecha* of going into himself and learning about the weaknesses of his own character. What do you think of this? Would it ultimately be a good strategy for Abram and the nation that was to come?

3 Leon Kass sums up this deception, saying that 'a wife is not transmutable into a sister or a concubine when it suits one's purpose'. Do you agree? What do you think of the comment, 'True affirmation of relationships is one of life's most important lessons'? In what ways do you think this may be true? Did Abram learn the lesson? Have you?
4 Abram seemed to have little sense that his mission in life was meant to be a joint venture with Sarai. Why could Abram and Sarai's trip to Egypt not be considered a joint venture? If you are married, what possibilities are open to you and your spouse?
5 God had promised Abram a prosperous future. Yet when he arrived in Canaan and a famine came along, he continued on to Egypt, where he hoped to find food and pasture. There is no record of either him or Sarai praying to God for guidance in what was surely a critical situation. What do you make of this?
6 One might hope that Abram was profoundly embarrassed and thoroughly ashamed of his treatment of Sarai. What do you think? Does he seem like one who would feel remorse about this? Can you cite any evidence on his behalf?
7 In the Bible 'going down to Egypt' often entails acting in our own wisdom and strength without consulting the Lord and asking him for help. Have you ever 'gone down to Egypt'?

6
Abram and Lot

From Egypt to Bethel – the test of wealth (Gen. 13)

Abram returned to Bethel and called 'upon the name of the LORD' (v. 4). The possessions gained in Egypt led to tension between the herdsmen of Abram and Lot, and eventually to separation of the two.

- Abram gave Lot the choice of where to live. This raises the question of the implications of such choices for location, business, family, children and culture.
- Abram was not abandoned by God for his denial of Sarai. He retraced his steps and went back to where he had been before his wrong move.

Now Abram had to face some new challenges that arose because of his material wealth.

- God nowhere says that material possessions are wrong in themselves or unspiritual.
- He does warn us against setting our hope in them and failing to share them.

Over the years, both Abram and Lot had amassed large herds, and pressure for pasture space led to tensions between their herdsmen.

- Such tensions are common in families, especially concerning inheritance or favoritism.

It is important that believers resolve them appropriately. Abram, the older man, took the initiative in trying to sort things out.

- He recognized the importance of kinship.
- He had failed to do this with his wife Sarai.

Believers often fail in this important area. We are reminded in Scripture of our obligation.

- 'Am I my brother's keeper?' (Gen. 4.9).
- We should resolve differences together (1 Cor. 6.1–8).

In the West especially, our societies are increasingly litigious. Do we always have to assert our rights?

- Families and church brothers and sisters often go to court.
- Such wrangling undermines the credibility of the Church.
- Allowing things to fester can be deadly.

Conflict resolution is a skill that is much needed in the Church, including:

- how to adjudicate wisely between disputing parties;
- when to let things go and suffer the loss.

Here are some interesting notes regarding Abram and Lot's situation. There is no record of

- Lot deferring to Abram as his older relative;
- either of them seeking God's will in prayer.

Thus, Abram settled in the land of Canaan, while Lot settled among the cities of the valley and moved to Sodom.

Lot chose to settle near Sodom because it would provide good grazing for his herds. This looks like a good business choice and from a purely commercial perspective it probably was. But there are other perspectives that are important for believers:

- The men of Sodom had a reputation for sexual depravity.
- Lot soon discovered the cultural and moral influence.
- Tradition says that Lot's wife was a native of the region.

It was dangerous to move near Sodom then, and it is now as well. Sodom is only a click or two away in cyberspace from any of us.

Jesus and the apostles were willing to let some things go but were strong on confronting other things.

- Paul advised letting some financial disputes and lawsuits between believers go but he did not suggest that the Corinthians should let sexual transgressions go (1 Cor. 6).
- Peter did not let Ananias and Sapphira's deception go (Acts 5.1–11).
- Jesus taught that we are not to judge others, but told us to be aware of false prophets (Matt. 7).

Thus, we need to ensure that our judgements are fair and we must be willing to let some things go and to confront other things. God would test Abram on the moral issue later.

From Bethel to Mamre (Gen. 13.14–18)

Abram moved to Mamre near Hebron and built another altar there.

Next, God appeared to Abram and spoke with him about the extent of his inheritance and his progeny.

- He was to inherit all the land he saw.
- His descendants would inherit all of it.

Abram built an altar to show that he viewed these appearances of God as having permanent value – something tangible to remember that they had happened, and where.

Abram's two tests thus far – how to cope with famine on the one hand and with wealth and plenty on the other – may well face us at some time or other. Paul's advice is useful here (Phil. 4.10–14).

- The secret of Paul's ability was his relationship with the Lord.
- Abram had not progressed to Paul's level, but he had begun.

The battle of the kings: the test of responsibility

Lot was caught up in a battle between groups of Babylonian and Canaanite kings, which included the king of Sodom.

When the Canaanite coalition was defeated by the Babylonian group, Lot was captured with his possessions.

- One of the escapees reported to Abram.
- Abram had a decision to make about Lot.
- Up to this point, there is little evidence of people taking real moral responsibility.

When Abram learned that Lot had been taken captive, he led his trained men, 318 of them, in pursuit all the way to Dan.

- Who were these 318 men? Apparently, Abram had bought them. They were slaves. They had certain limited rights and could be given great responsibility, unlike more recent slaves.
- Other allies included Abram's friends: Aner, Eshcol, Mamre and their men.
- What was the outcome? They mounted a night attack, routed the Babylonian oppressors and rescued Lot and his household.

After the rescue, Abram had a couple of important visitors:

- the king of Sodom, who offered Abram the spoils;
- Melchizedek, the king of Salem and priest of God, who blessed Abram and gave him one tenth of the spoils. (See next chapter.)

Abram's standing in the region must have been greatly enhanced. Was he beginning to be a blessing in the world?

This is the first time in Scripture where a believer is actively involved in battle. Here are some important points to remember when discussing the morality of war:

- We know that Jesus did not come to earth to set up a kingdom like modern-day countries (John 18.36).
- The apostle Paul taught, 'Though we walk in the flesh, we are not waging war according to the flesh' (2 Cor. 10.3).
- There is one set of moral commandments repeated in the Old and New Testaments.
- There is no indication Abram discussed Lot's rescue with God. However, he was blessed by the priest of God afterwards.

Application questions

1 The settling of the pasture dispute doesn't appear to have been a spiritual decision at all – it was the way non-believers might settle a dispute. Abraham gave Lot first choice and Lot picked the best land. No prayer, no discussion, no talk of future relations. A cut-and-dried business decision. What do you think?
2 We are all aware that family tensions are common. What about your extended family? Are there any tensions there? How do you go about resolving inheritance or favouritism challenges? Do prayer and discussion play a role? Should they?
3 Conflict resolution is badly needed in the Church today – the ability to adjudicate between disputing parties. Is it always right to confront things? Can it sometimes be right to let things go? Have you had any experience with letting things go to your disadvantage? How did that turn out?
4 The name Sodom has come to stand for evil and wickedness. Do you think Lot took the place's reputation into account when he made his choice of land? Have you ever found yourself in morally 'dangerous territory'? If you are willing, share any lessons you learned from the experience.
5 Abram was quick to intervene when Lot was captured by Babylonian troops. He was certainly in grave danger from a physical or bodily

perspective. One wonders if Abraham should have intervened earlier, when Lot moved to Sodom and exposed himself to moral danger. What do you think? What might Abram have done?

6 Abram's penchant for building altars is explained well here and is instructive for us. He built them, we are told, to give a sense of permanence to the appearances of God's presence he had experienced and to mark the physical locations of the appearances. What about you? Have you erected any altars to give permanence to God's dealing with you? Can you share anything about them?

7
Abram and Melchizedek

Abram and the aftermath

After his return from the defeat of the kings who had captured Lot, Abram met Melchizedek king of Salem and priest of God Most High. He served Abram bread and wine and blessed him.

Evidence that Melchizedek was superior to Abram:

- Melchizedek blessed Abram.
- Abram gave him a tenth 'of everything'.

In contrast, the king of Sodom

- curtly ordered Abram to give him the people Abram had freed from the enemy;
- gratefully offered Abram the material possessions.

This raises the question of the importance of material possessions.

- Gratitude dictated that those who helped should be compensated.
- How could Abram allow Lot to go back to Sodom if he really cared for him?
- Were the spoils of war God's way of making Abram's name great?
- If Abram had accepted the offer of the spoils, he would have been indebted to the king of Sodom.

Resisting the temptation to be made rich by others is an important life principle. The people of God must be careful about doing anything that hints at covetousness and self-serving.

The New Testament letter to the Hebrews draws our attention to the meaning of the name Melchizedek.

- The name itself: 'king (*melekh*) of righteousness (*tsadiq*)', or 'my king (*melchi*) is righteous'.
- The name of the city over which he ruled, Salem (*shalom*), means 'peace'. Some think Salem was Jerusalem.

The theme of righteousness is foundational to biblical thought.

- It is an Aramaic term meaning 'straight, even, speaking the truth'.
- It refers to characteristics of uprightness, integrity, truthfulness, justice and transparency in thought, word and deed, both privately and publicly.

This incident in Abram's life has to do with the relationship of peace to righteousness. Abram

- tried to restore peace and harmony between his herdsmen and those of Lot;
- separated from Lot and his people to do so;
- got mixed up in international conflict and used force to rescue Lot.

Up to this point, Abram had signally failed.

- He had been duplicitous with regard to his wife in Egypt.
- His wealth had increased, causing a problem.
- He had not steered Lot away from seductive Sodom.

Did he discuss the matters of truth and righteousness with Melchizedek?

Melchizedek is an important figure.

- He is the first person in Scripture to be called a priest.

- He was designated as priest of the Most High God using the term El Elyon for God (the Most High God or God of Israel).
- Abram apparently considered him a priest of the one true God, not of *a* god. Thus, their meal together was a feast of a fellowship of believers.

King David mentions Melchizedek in Psalm 110, where he writes of the Messiah, 'You are a priest for ever after the order of Melchizedek' (v. 4). Up to this point, there had only been the Levitical order of priesthood.

- Jesus, addressing the Pharisees nearly a thousand years after David wrote, asked them, 'If then David calls him Lord, how is he his son?' (Matt. 22.45).
- They agreed that the Messiah would be a descendant of David and they understood that 'sitting at God's right hand' implied divinity. Jesus' argument shows that the Messiah would be a human descendant of Abraham and David, and would be more than human. He would be God.
- Peter echoed this statement saying: 'Let all the house of Israel therefore know for certain that God has made him both Lord and Christ, this Jesus whom you crucified' (Acts 2.36).

The provision of divine help: Jesus as our High Priest

There are two orders of priests mentioned in Scripture:

- that of Aaron and Levi, instituted in Exodus to take charge of Israel's worship and service in connection with the tabernacle;
- that of Melchizedek, which existed prior to the Levitical priesthood.

Genesis is a book where all prominent figures are given a genealogy. Their deaths and ages at death are described. But no such details are given for Melchizedek. How are we to explain this omission?

In light of the record in Hebrews, this omission was deliberate.

- Melchizedek suddenly appeared at a point where his ministry was needed, and then disappeared.
- Melchizedek is a model of Jesus as an eternal High Priest available to help in times and places of need.

Thus, the order of Melchizedek is very different from the order of Levi.

- Levi's order engaged thousands of priests through time.
- Melchizedek's order engaged two: Melchizedek and the Lord Jesus, the Messiah.

And it is important to note that the mention of Melchizedek in the New Testament is to give authentication, particularly to Jewish people, that a different order of priesthood relating to the Messiah was not a Christian innovation; it had already been predicted in the Old Testament in Psalm 110.

Just as Melchizedek was there at the right time to support and strengthen Abram, so the Lord Jesus will be there for us.

In order to appreciate the practical implications of this material, we need to set it in the original context of the letter to the Hebrews.

- It was written to Christian believers of Jewish heritage.
- They were under increasing pressure to give up claims that Jesus was the Messiah and turn back to the old Jewish ways and priesthood.

The writer urges them to stand firm in their belief of Jesus as the Messiah, the Son of God.

The material in the letter to the Hebrews compares and contrasts

- the old Jewish system instituted by Moses, with sanctuary, sacrifices and ritual, with
- the system Jesus initiated, with a new sanctuary, a new sacrifice – all of which are superior to the old in every way.

The heart of Christianity is that the Lord Jesus made provision for the guilt of our sin on the cross; that he rose for our justification and sent the Holy Spirit to indwell us and develop our new life.

- Many people think that faith is given by God to those he arbitrarily chooses – one has it, another doesn't.
- Others think very differently. They hold that one of God's gracious gifts to all men and women as creatures made in his image is the capacity to believe and thus form genuine relationships, in particular by opening their hearts and minds to put their whole trust in Christ.

How are you going to stand for truth tomorrow with all the opposition you will face?

- Long ago, Melchizedek was sent to Abram to be his high priest.
- In a similar way, Jesus now acts as our High Priest, supporting us in prayer and presence through his Spirit.

Observe how Jesus spoke to Peter at the Last Supper:

- Jesus told him that Satan wanted to sift him like wheat.
- Peter thought his faith was strong enough and asserted his readiness to follow.
- Jesus predicted that, instead of standing with him, Peter would deny him three times.
- Jesus prayed for Peter and ensured that his *faith* did not fail.

The king of Sodom was an evil man and no doubt Melchizedek's intervention saved Abram from harm.

- The ill-gotten riches of Sodom could easily have become a root of all kinds of evil for Abram.
- Jesus taught that life does not consist in what we have above and beyond what we need.
- And further, what we have can't extend our lives; nor can worrying about our possessions.

'For what does it profit a man to gain the whole world and forfeit his soul?' (Mark 8.36). Life trumps goods.

If we put the ideas of rule, righteousness and attitude towards goods together, we are reminded of the Sermon on the Mount.

- Jesus taught that we are not to worry about things necessary for life.
- We are to seek first the kingdom of God and his righteousness, and all these things will be given to us.

For the believer, material things are the by-product of work, not the goal.

- The goal is to seek the kingdom of God; and
- to live out the fundamental confession 'Jesus is Lord'.

Paul wrote, 'For the kingdom of God is not a matter of eating and drinking but of righteousness and peace and joy in the Holy Spirit' (Rom. 14.17).

Abram now resolutely refuses to increase his wealth through his rescue of Lot. He now has a healthy attitude towards wealth. So should we.

- If God has blessed us in this way, we should use it for good.
- We need to consult our High Priest about our finances.

Application questions

1. We have looked very closely at this individual, Melchizedek, in the present chapter. What have you learned about Melchizedek (and/or Jesus) through this study?
2. How important are material possessions? This question is asked in the text, and our tendency might be to continue reading to find the textbook answer. But it will be helpful to answer the question before moving ahead. How important are material possessions to you? Are they a major concern, driving much of your decision-making, or are they just one of many considerations in your life?
3. Abram's encounter with Melchizedek addresses the relationship between peace and righteousness. It has been suggested that Abram

discussed the relationship of truth and righteousness with the priest. Is there any change in Abram's character that would suggest he did?

4 'Melchizedek suddenly appeared at a point where his ministry was needed, and then disappeared' suggests that Melchizedek is a model (type) of Jesus as an eternal High Priest, available to help us in times and places of need. This is good news! Have you thought of Jesus before in terms of his role as your High Priest? Will this change your way of thinking?
5 We are told that the book of Hebrews compares and contrasts the old Jewish system instituted by Moses with the system instituted by Jesus. And the message of Hebrews in this context is that every element in the system of Jesus – sanctuary, sacrifice and priesthood – is superior to the old in every way. Can you elaborate?
6 It is important to correct a wrong impression that many have regarding the issue of salvation. Many people believe that faith is given by God to those he arbitrarily chooses, so that one has it and another doesn't – and they can do nothing about it. The truth is that faith is the act of opening our hearts and minds to trust Jesus. How would you explain this to someone who is confused?
7 In the Sermon on the Mount, Jesus encourages us not to worry about things necessary for life. God will supply these as we need them. We are to seek his kingdom and his righteousness, and allow him to attend to everything else. Are you following this priority scheme in your life? Is it working?

8
Justification by faith

Sometime after the rescue of Lot, God spoke again to Abram and promised him great reward.

- Abram had plenty of material wealth.
- He had been in the land 25 years, but still he had no heir to share the blessings.
- God recognized Abram's unspoken turmoil, so he invited him to look at the night sky, and count the stars if he was able. That was how many descendants he would have.

What was Abram to say? He had already been promised a child at least four times. Could he continue to believe God's promise?

- He decided to continue to trust what God had said.
- And we are told, '[Abram] believed the LORD and he counted it to him as righteousness' (Gen. 15.6).

The Hebrew root word for faith is *aman*.

- It conveys the notion of trust and firmness, particularly trust in a person.
- This statement, connecting Abram's faith in God with righteousness, lies at the heart of the central biblical doctrine of justification by faith.

What is faith?

The account of God's call does not use the word 'faith'. Instead of telling us what was in Abram's mind, it tells us what he did.

- 'Abram went, as the Lord had told him' (Gen. 12.4).
- His faith is evidenced by his actions.

A passage in Hebrews gives us some insights into the nature of Abram's faith (11.8–10).

- Abram's faith was placed in God. Jesus remarked, 'Abraham rejoiced that he would see my day' (John 8.56).
- Abram believed that God would deliver on his promises of offspring and the land.
- Abram's faith was evidence-based, God's appearances and answers being the evidence he saw.

Since Abraham is presented to us in the New Testament as the example of what it means to trust God, it is worth spending time trying to understand precisely what faith is. Unfortunately, there are many today who believe faith is a purely religious concept that means believing where there is no evidence. For example:

- Bertrand Russell says that faith is 'the firm belief in something for which there is no evidence'.[26]
- Richard Dawkins says: 'Faith is a state of mind that leads people to believe something . . . in the total absence of supporting evidence.'[27]

To understand the origin of this erroneous view, we need to understand that faith has at least two meanings in common use:

- Faith in an objective sense refers to a collection of things to be believed, a set of teachings about facts and experience. For example, the Christian faith or the Jewish faith.
- Faith in the subjective sense is my faith or belief in facts, ideas and people; in God, in Christianity, in weather phenomena and a host of other things.

Everyone exercises faith every day in numerous ways.

- Some are adherents of a particular religious tradition.
- Then there is trust in maps, doctors, traffic lights and so on.

Faith in the second sense is not a religious concept.

Words used to communicate the notion of trustworthiness based on evidence are:

- *fides,* the Latin word from which we get 'fidelity';
- *pistis*, from *peitho*, meaning 'persuade' in the New Testament;
- *aman*, a Hebrew word conveying the idea of trust and firmness, particularly trust in a person.

Russell's and Dawkins' attempts to define faith are misleading and false.

- They focus on blind faith, or faith without evidence.
- They use faith and belief as two different concepts.

Whenever we see the word 'faith', we need to ask two questions:

- Where is the faith placed – in what or in whom?
- What are the grounds, the evidence, on which it is based?

Here is a good example. In John 20.30–31, John says that Jesus did many signs (miracles), and these were written (given) that we might believe that

- Jesus is the Christ (Messiah);
- Jesus is the Son of God.

And the result is that we may have life in his name.

Thus, the biblical concept of faith is neither credulous nor blind, but is a personal commitment based on evidence.

What is justification by faith?

Abram's experience of justification by faith is explained in detail in the New Testament and is relevant to all believers in Christ.

The Greek word used in the New Testament for 'righteous' can mean

- 'a person who observes custom, rule, right';
- 'judgment' in a legal sense.

The words translated 'justify' mean 'to declare righteous' or 'to confer a righteous status on'. They don't mean 'to make righteous'.

When we ask someone to justify something, we are not asking them to make it right, but to declare why it was or is right.

There has been ongoing theological controversy about whether the act of justification refers to

- the conferment of righteous status upon someone; or
- making someone ethically righteous by moral regeneration.

It is clear that both justification and moral transformation (sanctification) are of paramount importance, and that understanding the relationship between the two is crucial.

- First justification
- Then sanctification.

What gives the gospel message its saving power is that it originates with God. The person who puts their faith/trust in God through Christ is

- justified (declared righteous before God);
- sanctified (develops moral character, by the Holy Spirit).

What starts in faith continues to grow through faith.

Some get confused here, thinking that the way to achieve a righteous status with God is to merit or earn it by

- keeping the moral law, e.g. the Ten Commandments;
- believing we can make up for any shortfall by increasing our effort.

This notion appeals to many in our merit-based culture.

One of the most important lessons from Abraham is that he was justified by faith alone – before the law of Moses existed. This came 430 years later (see Gal. 3.17–18, 29).

The gospel is the power of God: people need to be saved. Why should we believe that people are guilty?

- The evidence of creation – it is clear that God is the author of it.
- The moral law in their conscience.
- The testimony of Scripture.

These combine to condemn all of us without exception as falling short of God's standards.

The moral standards built into our conscience communicate to us the knowledge of sin. They measure how far short we fall. If we repent of (turn from) our sins and trust God,

- he confers a righteous status upon us;
- he acquits us of the guilt incurred by all our sins.

Paul uses the example of Abraham to establish this crucial legal principle (Rom. 4.1–2).

- He takes Abraham to be a historical person.
- He states that Abraham did not merit salvation.
- He shows that Abraham's justification was an undeserved gift of God's free grace, to be accepted in humility and gratitude.

God is interested in righteous behaviour. The secret of salvation is that

- it is a gracious gift received by faith;
- it leads to good works.

Application questions

1 God spoke to Abram, promising to shield him and to give him great reward. Abram, at this stage of his life, had great wealth, but he lacked children. Was Abram troubled here? What evidence can you suggest in support of this contention?

2 'Abraham believed God, and it was counted to him as righteousness' (Rom. 4.3) is certainly one of the most important passages in Scripture. What do you understand by this? How can it apply to our lives?

3 Abraham's faith was based on the evidence of God appearing to him and the fact that he kept his promises to him. Today, we have overwhelming evidence that the Scriptures are true and that God is who he says he is. Yet many people protest that there is no evidence. What evidence is your faith based on?

4 A long-running controversy in the Christian Church involves two very important doctrines: justification and sanctification. Can you explain the difference between these two ideas?

5 Part of the reason for the confusion between justification and sanctification is that much in society is merit-based. People are rewarded on the basis of what they accomplish in their entire lives. Does God operate a merit-based system when it comes to our relationship with him? Explain.

6 Paul also writes, 'for all have sinned and fall short of the glory of God' (Rom. 3.23). Can you explain what this has to do with justification by faith? Some think that, if we fall short, we just need to work a little harder and things will be fine. What is the problem with this logic? Is there a solution? What is it?

7 Is God interested in righteous behaviour? The secret of salvation is that it is a gracious gift received by faith and it leads to good works. Can you see evidence in your own life that the result of your faith in Jesus has been righteous behaviour? Could you share some of the things you have identified?

9

God's covenant with Abram

God now spoke to Abram about his inheritance of the promised land. But Abram said, 'O Lord GOD, how am I to know that I shall possess it?' (Gen. 15.8).

All kinds of doubts and other concerns occupied Abram's mind.

- Warring factions were all around.
- The Babylonians and Canaanites were close by.

How could Abram be sure that this part of God's promise would be fulfilled? The answer: God made a covenant with him.

Throughout history, covenants – legally formalized documents – have been instruments designed to be security for signatories of such agreements. Examples are:

- financial documents
- property contracts
- marriage certificates.

God gave Abram a covenant *in perpetuity*, which is described in Genesis 15.9–21.

One way of ratifying covenants in the ancient Near East was to cut animals in half:

- two piles of halves were laid out on the ground;
- the 'signatories' walked between the piled halves, indicating that they were solemnly bound to keeping the covenant.

In Hebrew, this is called the covenant between the parts.

The prophet Jeremiah refers to this ritual (Jer. 34.18–19).

- In the covenant with Abram, he did not walk between the pieces, since he had no condition to fulfil. Only the presence of God moved between the pieces.
- In Jeremiah's covenant, the people ratified the agreement by walking between the parts.

We engage these days in so-called one-party covenants in the form of a last will or testament, wherein one party makes a formal commitment to others.

- These covenants are called one-party or unilateral even though more than one party is usually involved.
- A biblical example is God's covenant never to flood the earth again after Noah, signified by a rainbow.

In the case of the agreement with Abram in Genesis 15, one might have expected a ceremony representing conferment of great blessings. Instead, the scene was one of sacrifice, dread and darkness.

God announced that Abram would have offspring, but they would endure four centuries of oppression before inheriting the promised land and returning to it with great wealth.

God assured Abram that he personally would live to a good old age. But no mention was made of his living to enjoy the promised inheritance.

From our vantage point, we can see the connection between Abram's experience of darkness and the present evil of anti-Semitism:

- The bitter enemy of Abraham's race, expressed in genocidal attempts to eliminate the Jews and culminating in the twentieth century with the Holocaust.
- There is evidence that anti-Semitism is rising again in Europe and elsewhere. We must not allow that to happen – but how can we stop it?

Subsequent history has confirmed the prediction contained in terms of the covenant with Abram and thus becomes part of the evidence for the truth and reliability of Scripture.

Application questions

1. We make many covenants today in our culture. There are different kinds of purchase agreements, business transactions, partnership agreements and so on. But these are usually rather sterile events, where we walk into an office, sign some paperwork, take a copy and walk out. This is a bit different from the covenant in which Abram was involved. Imagine enacting a covenant with God! Have you ever done this? What was the nature of the covenant?
2. The agreement Abram concluded with God was huge in terms of its provisions. It is suggested that the magnitude of the blessings promised was such that one would have reasonably expected a celebration on Abram's part. But there was none. Instead, there was a sense of darkness and horror. Explain why this was so.
3. We are warned in the concluding paragraphs of the chapter that the suffering is not over yet. Jews have been, are being and will continue to be persecuted around the world. Also, persecution of Christians is increasing even now. But the end is assured. Our inheritance is guaranteed by the resurrection of Jesus. Saints, under the rule of Christ, will rule the earth! Does this give you courage? How?

10
The new covenant

Two covenants – the old and the new

The distinction between one- and two-party covenants differentiates between what we call the old and the new covenants.

- The covenant between God and Abraham was a one-party covenant, ratified by God alone. The new covenant later instituted by Jesus in the Upper Room with his disciples was a one-party covenant ratified by Christ alone.
- The old covenant made by God at Sinai with the Jews was a two-party covenant.

The differences between one-party and two-party covenants has led to confusion and tension between Jews and Christians and between various Christian traditions.

The covenant at Sinai had as its basis the law of Moses.

- The people covenanted to keep all the words of the law, but they soon discovered that they could not keep God's laws and so they broke their side of the covenant agreement.
- God then instituted a system of animal sacrifices and offerings to teach the people the need for repentance to cover their guilt and restore fellowship with God.
- But this was only a temporary solution – the blood of bulls and goats could never take away sin.

The prophet Jeremiah recognized that there was a problem with that first covenant (Jer. 31.31–32). It was a two-party covenant and the people broke their side of it.

Stepping back for historical perspective, we have:

1 The covenant with Abraham: a one-party covenant ratified by God.
2 The covenant with Israel: a two-party covenant between God and Israel.
3 The new covenant: a one-party covenant ratified by Christ.

One question that arises is: if covenant 2 did not negate covenant 1, why was there a need for covenant 3? We will cover this later.

For now, we note that Abram's security and the security of believers in Christ lie in the priority of God's covenant 1 with Abram over covenant 2.

Paul argues in Galatians 3:15–18, 29 that the promise in covenant 1 was given to Abraham and his offspring (singular, i.e. Jesus).

- The promise was made before the law of Moses, and the law has no power to invalidate the original promise.
- This is no mere detail in the story, since it has far-reaching implications for believers in Christ.
- If we are Christ's, we are Abraham's offspring and heirs according to the promise!

And faith is the basis for being accounted as righteous before God. The inheritance is not earned by efforts to keep the law. Paul affirms this in Romans 4.13–16.

What does this have to do with us? Everything!

- Those of us who trust Christ are offspring of Abraham.
- From a legal perspective, we are irrevocably inheritors of the world.

Paul had to remind the Corinthian church of this (1 Cor. 6.2).

The word 'regeneration' has two meanings in the New Testament:

- the resurrection of the dead at Christ's return;
- the new birth through God's Holy Spirit by faith.

Our inheritance is reserved for us in heaven, guaranteed by the resurrection of Jesus, but we are not there yet. We are warned of trials to come.

The new covenant of Christ

The letter to the Hebrews (chapter 10) clearly shows the superiority of the new covenant over the old covenant, leading to several questions:

- Why is there any need for a new covenant?
- How could God accept Abraham simply because he trusted God?

Consider the original readers of the letter.

- Their ancestors died without ever hearing about the new covenant.
- They brought animal sacrifices to atone for their sin, but did they really get forgiveness, or not?

Animal sacrifices could never take away sin; they foreshadowed the way in which God would eventually deal with sin through the sacrifice of Jesus.

The sacrifice of Jesus works backwards in time as well as forwards, so God could righteously deal with the sins of those who lived before Jesus died (Rom. 3.21–26).

- Sin is universal. All have sinned and fall short of the glory of God.
- Humans are justified on the basis of the death of Christ.

So how can God pass over sins committed by individuals who lived before Christ? He counted their faith in him as righteousness, knowing that Jesus would eventually come and die for their sins.

How much did Abraham understand about this? John suggests an answer (John 8.56):

- 'Abraham rejoiced that he would see my day.'
- 'He saw it and was glad.'

Another question is: does it make any difference whether one lives before the death and resurrection of Jesus or afterwards? The short answer is yes. Consider the tabernacle that Moses set up, or the Temple built by Solomon.

- Each had two compartments separated by a veil. The first compartment was called the holy place; the second was called the holy of holies. It was a symbol of God's presence among his people.
- The priests in Israel ministered daily in the first compartment; the high priest once a year on Yom Kippur in the second (Heb. 9.6–10).

This indicates that the way into the most holy place was not freely open as long as these compartments were still divided by the veil.

And the implication is that the gifts and sacrifices were only in effect until a better system (the sacrifice of Jesus) was established.

The old system was reformed when Jesus came.

- He entered once and for all into the holy place, not by means of the blood of animals but by his own blood.
- He is the mediator of a new covenant.

Christ's offering of himself does what the animal sacrifices could not do – purify the conscience. And the result is that

- people in New Testament times and later, who put their faith in God through Jesus, are counted as righteous on the basis of Jesus' death;
- people in Old Testament times, who put their faith in God knowing little about Jesus, are also counted as righteous because of his death.

The new covenant for Christians

During the week in which he was crucified, Jesus celebrated the Passover.

- He had entered Jerusalem triumphantly earlier.
- The leaders were threatened by his claim to be the Messiah.

Jesus (the King Messiah) sat at the table with his disciples (his subjects).

- After finishing the meal, he offered them a cup which he said was a new covenant in his blood.
- It would lead to their occupying thrones as rulers in Israel (Luke 22.14–20, 28–30).

Later, Paul authoritatively said that the new covenant applied to all believers in Christ (1 Cor. 11.23–26).

Throughout his life, Abraham must have reflected on

- the night God said he was justified by faith;
- the night when God made the covenant with him;
- when God promised him offspring and an inheritance.

Those of us who have likewise been justified by our faith in the Lord Jesus should also reflect on our experience by celebrating the Lord's Supper. Taking the bread and wine do not convey salvation. We take them because

- we have already received salvation;
- we wish to express our gratitude to Jesus as our Saviour, and our commitment to him as Lord.

The symbols point to the basis of the covenant and represent his body and blood. He died for our sins.

Taking the cup means we are consciously pledging ourselves to accept Jesus as Lord of our lives according to the terms of the covenant. Two facts are important:

- the new covenant replaces only the Sinai covenant;
- it was necessary because Israel broke its agreement.

The letter to the Hebrews sets out the terms of the new covenant, citing Jeremiah 31.33–34.

- 'I will . . . write [my laws] on their hearts';
- 'They shall all know me, from the least of them to the greatest';

- 'I will remember their sins no more'.

Instead of using stone tablets, the laws are written on our hearts.
God is righteous and he wants us to be righteous:

- not only by being right with God by faith in Christ;
- but also by living righteous, morally upright lives.

He invites us to trust him

- to justify us by faith;
- to supply the power to live by his standards.

When we take the cup, we are asking God to go on writing those laws on our heart, mind and conscience.

The Lord's Supper is designed as an instrument to help us grasp the glory of this good news and to understand God's provision for our growth in character and integrity.

Before we take the cup, we should examine ourselves to see if there is any unconfessed sin, and then repent. The Greek word for repent is *metanoia*, meaning:

- a fundamental change of mind about our sin;
- repudiating and turning away from our sin with God's help.

The command to remember the Lord in the communion service forces us into the discipline of

- examining our lives;
- repenting before God;
- acknowledging Jesus' death on the cross as the only source of forgiveness and restoration;
- accepting his forgiveness with gratitude.

Application questions

1. We need to take care that we don't confuse the old and new covenants by not paying attention to what constitutes 'old' and 'new'. Can you explain the difference? How was Jesus able to institute the new covenant?
2. When Moses brought the commandments written on the stone tablets from Mount Sinai, the people quickly agreed to keep them all. It didn't take long for them to discover that keeping the law is impossible. So, what is the solution?
3. The letter to the Hebrews is important for our understanding of the covenants in Scripture. Why was there any need for a new covenant?
4. 'The sacrifice of Christ works backwards in time as well as forwards, so God could righteously deal with the sins of those who lived before Jesus died.' Do you understand this? Explain it in your own words.
5. Jesus said to a group of people in the Temple, 'Your father Abraham rejoiced that he would see my day. He saw it and was glad' (John 8.56). Explain this in the light of what we have seen in considering the new covenant.
6. In speaking of the holy places we learn that Jesus entered once and for all into the holy places; not by means of the blood of animals, but by means of his own blood. This clearly demonstrates that Jesus is the mediator of a new covenant that replaces the old one. Why is this a significant point in God's relationship with humans?
7. Paul wrote in 1 Corinthians 11.23–26 that the new covenant applies to all believers in Christ. Why did it have to be this way?
8. The discussion of the Lord's Supper is particularly encouraging. 'Taking the cup means we are consciously pledging ourselves to accept Jesus as Lord of our lives according to the terms of the covenant.' What are the terms of the new covenant?
9. The Ten Commandments were originally engraved on stone tablets. We are told by Jeremiah that, under the new covenant, God will write his laws upon our hearts. This is a beautiful picture of what God has done. Can you cite any evidence that God has actually done this in your own heart?

Part 3

GENESIS 16.1—19.38

11
A surrogate son

Hagar the surrogate

In the first part of this section, Sarai despairs of having her own children.

- Many women today have to cope with infertility, but in the ancient world it was a mark of failure.
- This is the first time we see Sarai talking to her husband.
- In Egypt, Abram asked her to compromise the meaning of 'wife' by posing as his sister.
- Here Sarai asks Abram to compromise the meaning of 'child' by employing a surrogate.
- Sarai tells Abram that the Lord is responsible for her infertility.
- She does not enlist her husband to take the matter before the Lord in prayer.
- Genesis is silent about how much Abram engaged with his faith to comfort Sarai in her situation.

Waiting on the Lord's timing is one of the great themes of Scripture.

- 'Wait for the LORD and keep his way' (Ps. 37.34).
- 'They who wait for the LORD shall renew their strength' (Isa. 40.31).

These verses are easy to read but may be difficult to put into practice.

- We think we know what God intends to do.
- When nothing happens, we step in to help.

Sarai suggested to Abram that he take Hagar as a concubine/wife to be a surrogate mother.

- This was not uncommon in Old Testament times.
- Though by different means, it is increasingly common today.

Hagar was probably given to Sarai by Pharaoh when she was in Egypt.
The story reflects some remarkable anti-symmetry.

- In Egypt, Abram pressured Sarai to deny her true relationship with him. She agreed and was taken into Pharaoh's harem.
- Here, Sarai pressures Abram to deny her true relationship with him and take another partner, the servant girl Hagar. Abram obliges Sarai.

Their motives were also questionable.

- In Egypt, Abram was motivated by fear and the desire for wealth.
- Here, Sarai is motivated by shame at her infertility and willingness to seize any solution.

In neither episode did Abram and Sarai show any interest in the consequences for their own relationship.

- Sarai's plan meant that Abram's child would have an Egyptian mother.
- Abram's plan risked that Sarai's child would have an Egyptian father.

We are informed here that the man listened to his wife without either of them consulting the Lord. Adam had done the same thing.

It will be useful to pursue further the similarities between Sarai and Abram and Adam and Eve.

- In Genesis 3, Eve took the forbidden fruit.
  - She offered it to her husband Adam.
  - Adam took it so as not to refuse Eve.

- Here, Sarai took her slave girl.
  - She offered her to her husband Abram.
  - Abram took her so as not to refuse Sarai.

In a real sense, Sarai and Abram re-enacted the Fall.

- One consequence of the Fall was that childbearing became problematic and painful.
- What Abram and Sarai did led to a 'knowledge of good and evil' they would live to regret.

When Hagar became pregnant, she began to despise Sarai – she realized that infertility had been Sarai's problem, not Abram's.

We now have a two-way discussion between a husband and wife, the first in the Bible.

- Sarai had expected servile co-operation. She discovered instead that Hagar was a real human with feelings and ambitions of her own.
- Sarai felt threatened and called upon the Lord to judge between them.
- Abram responded by telling Sarai to do with Hagar as she liked and use her as a means to Sarai's ends.

It was unquestionably a tragic dereliction of his role as husband and father.

Abram and Sarai would face bitter lessons about what can happen when you use others to accomplish your own ends.

- Surrogacy gave rise to deep psychological and moral issues.
- It was not compatible with God's design for them.
- Everyone lost in the process.

Ros Clarke says: 'Infertility makes Sarai desperate and destructive. She jeopardises her marriage, forces another woman into having sex with her husband and then drives her . . . into the wilderness.'[28]

What happened to Hagar?

- She did not get far before her reserves were exhausted.

- But God cared for her and intervened.
  - Hagar named her son Ishmael ('God hears').
  - Hagar named the well where she encountered the angel *Beer-lahai-roi* ('the well of the living one who sees me').

God hears and God sees

The meaning of *El Roi* ('a God of seeing') reverberate down the centuries into our contemporary world.

God sees us at home, at work, on the internet and when we are alone in a hotel. He also sees us when we are

- bullied;
- disliked on social media;
- rejected by our friends.

There are no secrets from God.

Hagar, like many women, found herself in a very unpleasant and difficult place through no fault of her own. But God was and is concerned. He is more interested in the despised and rejected than we sometimes think.

When people make their decisions, expend their energy and try to live independently of God, they are living according to the flesh.

The flesh is the gravitational pull of our sinful nature that tries to pressure us into compromising our moral integrity. This happened to Abram, not before he was justified by faith, but afterwards. Paul describes it in Romans 7.15–25.

- Paul wanted to follow the law of God.
- He tried with his will, intellect and emotions.
- It wasn't enough.

It is here that we often get discouraged.

- We may have been believers for years.
- We find the pull of our fleshly nature too strong.

Living by faith in God means that we need to learn to depend on God's Spirit actively and consciously.

Thirteen years passed between the end of Genesis 16 and the beginning of chapter 17.

- During this time, Sarai, Abram and Hagar had to live with the consequences of their actions 'in the flesh'.
- In later centuries, much of the wandering and delay of Israel entering the land was caused by not living by faith.

Ishmael's growth into his teen years is not recorded in Scripture. It was prophesied that his hand would be against every man.

- Genesis relates some of what happened to Abraham's family, but it does not attempt to reflect, analyse or apply any details for future generations.
- In each generation, parenting demands a humble dependence on the mercy, grace, power and presence of God. We all start as 'beginner' parents.

Coping with infertility

The Bible draws our attention to the distress caused by infertility.

- Several examples from the Old and New Testaments are given, including Rachel and Jacob.
- The outcomes are jealousy, rivalry, favouritism and inevitable discord within the family.

The desire for children is a powerful, created instinct, so our response to infertility must be understanding and compassion over the brokenness of our world.

What about medical intervention?

- Some argue that, if a certain technology helps to produce children, we should use it.

- Others say that, just because we have the technology, it doesn't mean it is always morally right to use it.

It is always healthy to seek God's input on this.

What about surrogacy? Many believe that it is in a child's best interests to be born into a natural family structure in which family blood relationships have not been intentionally confused. The child and the surrogate mother (the most vulnerable ones and the ones most likely to be harmfully affected) may receive little or no protection.

Application questions

1. It is interesting and typical that Sarai blamed God for her infertility. As it turned out, she was not infertile; she would later give Abram his son Isaac. The problem here was that she was not willing to trust God's timing for her needs. Do we ever do this today? Do you have any examples?
2. So Sarai decided to 'help' God with her problem of childlessness. She suggested to Abram that he sleep with the servant girl Hagar, so that Sarai could have a surrogate child. How silly it is to think that she (or we) could possibly help God with his agenda. There is no indication that they took the matter before God to hear from him. What were the consequences of this?
3. Neither in Egypt, where Abram had Sarai pose as his sister, nor in Canaan, where Abram had sexual relations with Hagar, did either Abram or Sarai consider the harmful effects these actions would have on their own relationship. Could such discussions have changed things?
4. The outcomes from Sarai's and Abram's experience of using Hagar as a surrogate were unexpected and not good. We can all probably cite some examples of situations with unexpected outcomes. And we are probably all familiar with examples where things worked out. Have you ever tried to 'help' God with his plans? What happened?
5. One thing we do know is that we should not use others to accomplish our own ends. The case of Sarai and Hagar is a clear example of what can happen when we offend in this regard. We need constantly to

assess our motives in all of our relations with other people. Do you do this? How is it working?

6 God hears and God sees. Hagar was in a better position once God sent the angel to talk with her. This is a really encouraging turn of events. Can you give some examples of God seeing and hearing all that is going on in your life?
7 Be sure to read up thoughtfully on using medical technology and surrogacy to deal with the issue of infertility. Most of us probably haven't thought through these things because we haven't had to. We need to have a 'moral vision, shaped by a Christian understanding of the person and family'. How do we gain such an understanding?

12
The covenant of circumcision

God appeared again to Abram to establish an everlasting covenant with him and his offspring.

- First, he changed Abram's name (meaning 'exalted father') to Abraham (meaning 'father of many nations').
- This is the first name change we read of in Scripture.

God speaks as if that had already been accomplished – another evidence of the certainty of his promises.

- This hints at the fact that many individuals would regard Abraham as their progenitor.

God would now institute a further covenant with Abraham. It is called the covenant of circumcision because the surgical procedure of circumcision was its emblem.

Certain characteristics of this covenant are prominent.

- Circumcision was for male infants only.
- It was normally performed by fathers on newborn sons.
- It involved a strong commitment to keep the covenant.
- It encouraged men to take their responsibility as husbands and fathers seriously, integrating their children into God's purposes.
- It encouraged parents to take their vows seriously, including their vows to teach their children.

Circumcision in the Old and New Testaments

Circumcision was a physical mark applied to all of Abraham's physical posterity.

- It was a graphic way of teaching Abraham and his offspring not to put their trust in the flesh at the moral and spiritual level.
- It was a symbol to represent an underlying moral and spiritual attitude to reality.

Circumcision was always intended to convey something deeper than physical attributes. Consider the following:

- Jeremiah 9.25: 'those who are circumcised merely in the flesh . . . '
- Deuteronomy 30.6: 'The LORD your God will circumcise your heart . . . '

The key idea is that we need to cut the bad stuff out of our hearts – the works of the flesh.

Paul explained to the church in Rome:

- True Jewishness meant not only being circumcised but having spiritual convictions that were in accordance with the law of God (Rom. 2.25–29).
- Thus, the rite of physical circumcision did not make people spiritual children of Abraham.

Circumcision was a seal of the righteousness of faith that Abraham had while still uncircumcised.

- The purpose was to make him the father of all who believe without being circumcised.
- Abraham was first justified and then circumcised 13 years later.

Thus, justification has absolutely nothing to do with the rite of circumcision. Moreover, the law of Moses is not a means of justification either.

In spite of this reasoning, many people came to regard circumcision and keeping the law of Moses as the means of salvation. And, in a similar way, some regard baptism and communion as means of salvation.

The true circumcision

The New Testament calls circumcision at the spiritual level of transformative experience 'true circumcision'.

- 'We are the true circumcision, who worship God in spirit . . . and put no confidence in the flesh' (Phil. 3.3 RSV).
- 'For in Christ Jesus neither circumcision nor uncircumcision counts for anything, but only faith working through love' (Gal. 5.6).

The unregenerate heart cannot make itself love God. If ever we are to be able to love God, we must be cut loose from the flesh and be planted in the Spirit.

Paul uses the phrase 'in the flesh' to denote the unregenerate state.

- 'Those who are in the flesh cannot please God' (Rom. 8.8).
- Regeneration involves being in the Spirit.

When we repent and trust Christ, we are justified by faith. We are simultaneously changed by the Lord from being in the flesh and transplanted into the Spirit.

If we are believers in Christ:

- The roots of the flesh that held us down have been cut by the Lord himself.
- An important consequence of that is that we do not have to give in to the flesh.
- 'Walk by the Spirit, and you will not gratify the desires of the flesh' (Gal. 5.16).

What happened to Sarai? God's next action was focused on her. He changed her name

- from Sarai, an older Hebrew form,
- to Sarah, a newer Hebrew form.

Both mean 'princess'. She is the only woman in the Bible whose name was changed by God.

God then informed Sarah that she would have a son.

- God insisted that it would be Sarah who bore Abraham's son. This had to be, in order for the child to qualify as a worthy transmitter of the covenants.
- God also insisted that his name would be Isaac, reflecting Abraham and Sarah's reaction (laughter) to the announcement that she would have a son.

What happened to Ishmael? God made the following pronouncements about him:

- 'I will make him fruitful and multiply him greatly.'
- 'He shall father twelve princes, and I will make him into a great nation' (Gen. 17.20–21).

Abraham entertains the angels

'And the Lord appeared to him by the oaks of Mamre, as he sat at the door of his tent' (Gen. 18.1).

Who were these three?

- Merely humans?
- Angels?
- Two angels and the Lord?

Abraham spoke as though the Lord was in the group. Regardless, he prepared a meal for the three.

This shows the importance of showing hospitality.

- Scripture in general stresses the importance of hospitality.

- In the early Church, there was a real sense of interdependence and fellowship.

One of the three visitors inquired after Sarah.

- 'Where is your wife, Sarah?'
- When informed that she was in the tent, the Lord said (he must have been in the group), 'I will return next year. She will have a son.'

Sarah laughed from inside the tent.

- The Lord asked why Sarah laughed. And Sarah denied that she had laughed.
- The Lord answered, 'Is anything too hard for the Lord?' This is a challenge for us to trust him more confidently.

Application questions

1 In this section we read that Abram had his name changed by God from Abram (exalted father) to Abraham (father of many nations) and we are told that this was a repetition of God's promise to Abram to give him an abundance of offspring. But this would only have been credible if it came to pass. How do you think Abraham felt about his change of name?
2 As Christians we no longer practice circumcision. Has infant baptism taken over the role of this practice in some denominations? How do the two practices compare?
3 The three individuals who appeared to Abraham (Gen. 18.1–2) as he sat at the door of his tent have proved a bit of a puzzle to many over the years. Who were these three? Merely humans? Or angels? Or two angels and God? What do Abraham's words lead us to conclude?
4 Just as God 'saw' Hagar, this passage demonstrates how he also 'saw' Sarah. She had been through incredibly trying circumstances, but God recognized this and put in motion the single thing that would restore her. He promised that she would bear Abraham a son in the coming year. Can you give any examples of where God has seen your pain and provided for you?

13
The judgement of Sodom

The fate of Lot in Sodom

We now consider the fate of Lot in the immoral city of Sodom.

Three individuals turned to leave Abraham's tent and looked down towards Sodom and Gomorrah. Then God engaged Abraham in a discussion about Sodom.

- He first informed Abraham why he chose him.
- Then he told Abraham about his intent to judge the evil of Sodom and asked him about the justice of such judgement.
- Jesus used the Flood of Noah and the judgement of Sodom to point to the fact of his future return in judgement (Luke 17:26–30).
- Just as Noah found favour in God's eyes, Abraham would too. Three times in Scripture, he is called the friend of God (2 Chron. 20.7; Isa. 41.8; Jas 2.23).

Abraham and God stood together here as they contemplated the morality of Sodom.

- If we are going to teach others what moral behaviour means, we need to learn it ourselves.
- In order for Abraham to teach his children how to behave, he needed to learn what righteousness and justice were.

God was about to discuss with Abraham righteousness and justice not simply at the personal level but in the context of a city-community.

As two of the men left, Abraham remained standing before the Lord.

- Abraham knew the Lord intended to judge Sodom.
- Abraham also knew that Lot and his family were there.

He must have wondered if the judgement would be indiscriminate, or if there was hope for Lot and his family.

What could or should Abraham say to God?

- Could he persuade God to preserve Lot?
- What reasoning could he use for this?

It is one thing to judge an individual, but what about an entire community? Abraham would not have wanted Lot to be harmed as 'collateral damage' in a comprehensive verdict.

So he asked the Lord a series of questions as one friend might ask another.

- 'Will you indeed sweep away the righteous with the wicked?'
- 'Suppose there are fifty righteous within the city.'

And God replied, 'If I find at Sodom fifty righteous in the city, I will spare the whole place for their sake.'

Abraham's appeal to God was based on his conviction that God would surely do what was just and right. Having secured the city if 50 righteous were found, Abraham argued the number down by increments, until they reached agreement at ten righteous.

- Abraham did not question that the city needed to be judged.
- He seemed to be concerned only with righteous people.
- What should become of the mass of unrighteous people? Should they be allowed to escape because of the righteousness of a few?

Was Abraham defending injustice?

The basic principle here is that Abraham had confidence that the Judge of all the earth would do right.

- Jesus entrusted himself to the righteous Judge (1 Pet. 2.23).
- We need also to have confidence in his judgement.

What happened to Sodom and Lot?

- Abraham was not told immediately, but there were signs.
- He could see smoke rising from Sodom and Gomorrah.
- He may have assumed that Lot perished in the city.

Abraham didn't realize that there could be a third option. He didn't foresee what eventually happened.

- The wicked city was destroyed.
- God provided a way of escape for the righteous.

Two final comments are appropriate here:

- God knows how to rescue the righteous (2 Pet. 2.7–9).
- God did not engage Abraham to judge the cities.

Lot 'entertains' the angels

When the angels arrived in Sodom, Lot was no longer camping near the city. He had a house in the city.

- He was sitting at the city gate, and he invited the new arrivals to his home.
- He served them a simple meal of flat bread (matzot).

There is no mention of Lot's wife at this point.

After the meal there was an uproar.

- A mob from the city was at Lot's door.
- They insisted that Lot bring the men out to them so they could have sexual relations with them.

Their own bodies were not sacred to the men of Sodom, nor were the bodies of the visitors.

The New Testament tells us that Lot himself was a profoundly unhappy and tormented man (2 Pet. 2.7–8).

- He had become immersed in a society so immoral that it had almost completely eroded his moral compass.
- It must have pained him to realize all he had lost by bartering his soul for life in Sodom.

Then he abdicated every last vestige of fatherly responsibility by suggesting that the crowd violate his own virgin daughters instead of his visitors.

Lot's prospective sons-in-law laughed at the idea of God's supernatural judgement

- as Abram and Sarai had laughed at the promise of God for a son;
- as the people of Noah's day had mocked the idea of coming judgement;
- as people of our day mock belief in Christ's supernatural miracles and resurrection.

And Lot himself didn't get it. The angels told him to escape the city with his wife and daughters.

- He hesitated, and pleaded to be allowed to stay in the little city of Zoar.
- He should have wanted to get as far away as possible from Sodom.

Instead, his moral desensitization had left him with no sense of shame or conviction regarding his behaviour.

There is a vivid contrast between Lot pleading for Zoar and Abraham pleading for Sodom.

- Lot's argument had to do with the size of the city.
- Abraham's was to do with the number of righteous people there.

In the New Testament, Peter uses God's judgement on those ancient cities to show what will happen to ungodly people in general (2 Pet. 2.17–22).

- Whatever overcomes a person, to that they are enslaved.

- If, after escaping the defilements of the world through the knowledge of Jesus Christ, they become entangled in them once more and are overcome, then the last state is worse than the first.

Peter is not talking here about true believers who, like himself, temporarily deny the Lord but then repent. He is talking about

- those who are unregenerate;
- those who, like Lot's wife, look back and return, thus showing where their heart really lies.

Jesus used Lot's wife as a warning of what would happen at his return at the judgement (Luke 17.28–37). And especially those who turned away from discipleship.

The cave: Lot's daughters and their children

One wonders what Abraham must have thought as he saw the smoke billowing from Sodom and Gomorrah. Yet God remembered Abraham and rescued Lot.

- This illustrates an important principle of God's justice (2 Pet. 2.7–10).
- Lot was a righteous man. He had been justified by faith.
- God rescued him, but he suffered a permanent loss.

God can rescue us if we err, but he may not remove the consequences of our behaviour.

Lot survived with his two daughters. They committed incest with him, using him as a surrogate husband. Children and inheritance meant more to them than their father.

Two babies were born, Moab and Ammon, who fathered nations that eventually became two of the most evil tribes in all of biblical history.

- The Israelites committed immorality with the women of Moab during the exodus from Egypt.
- Ammon became famous for sacrificing their children to the god Molech.

Here are some important lessons we can learn from the episode of Sodom and Gomorrah.

- We need to put our confidence in God, not in our flesh.
- We need to avoid the sins of the flesh characterized by the city of Sodom.
- We need to focus on walking in the Spirit.
- We need to show hospitality to strangers.

Application questions

1. The thoughts God had regarding his relationship with Abraham before engaging him in a conversation about Sodom reveal that he truly considered Abraham as his friend. 'Shall I hide from Abraham what I am about to do?' Do you see other things that point to a real friendship?
2. Friends typically share common interests. Think of some of your friendships. What are your common interests? God was contemplating the morality of Sodom and discussing that with Abraham. Was this a common interest they shared? Why?
3. We surmise that Abraham was concerned that God's judgement of Sodom and the resulting punishment would be indiscriminate – that Lot would be harmed as 'collateral damage' in a comprehensive verdict. What gives you reason to think that this would not have happened?
4. The basic principle here, we are told, is that the Judge of the universe will do right. Why is this important? God can do whatever he wants – can't he?
5. In 2 Peter 2.9 we read, 'The Lord knows how to rescue the godly from trials, and to keep the unrighteous under punishment until the day of judgement.' Does this reinforce your confidence that Lot was accorded justice in the judgement of Sodom? How so?
6. Having escaped from Sodom, you would think that Lot should have wanted to get as far away from it as possible. Why then did he plead to be allowed to stay in the little city of Zoar, one of the towns in the region of Sodom? What was he thinking? What do you imagine caused him to desire to stay in the area?

Part 4

GENESIS 20.1—22.19

14
Sarah and Hagar

Abraham denies Sarah as his wife

Abraham took up his nomadic life once more and moved on until he reached the small town of Gerar.

Again, he tried to protect himself by repeating the half-truth that Sarah was his sister.

- He risked imperilling the identity of his child with which Sarah was already pregnant.
- He had forgotten God's promise in Genesis 15 that he would be Abraham's shield.

The king of Gerar, Abimelech, sent for Sarah and took her as Pharaoh had done earlier. God's intervention was immediate and direct. Abimelech's conversation with God is familiar.

- It is similar to Abraham's conversation regarding Sodom.
- The issue is whether God would slay the innocent.

Abraham had earlier misjudged Pharaoh and now he misjudged Abimelech even more. Abimelech confronted Abraham by asking him to explain his motives.

Abraham confessed that he had done it because he felt there was no fear of God in Gerar. He erred on three counts:

On facts
- Thinking there was no fear of God among Abimelech's servants.

On values

- Rationalizing his denial of his relationship with Sarah by telling a half-truth.

On motives

- Asking Sarah to involve herself in the dishonest attempt to protect her husband.

And he also compromised on his calling. God had called him to witness to the one true God, Creator of heaven and earth.

This passage is a powerful message to us that we need to be very careful not to underestimate others – especially those who do not share our Christian commitment.

It is easy to make embarrassing mistakes in judging the ethics of others.

- Not all kings in the region were as dissolute and wicked as the king of Sodom.
- Abimelech appears to have been God-fearing to some extent. God cited the integrity of Abimelech's heart.

The first chapter of Genesis tells us that all people are made in the image of God.

- All of us have a conscience that instructs us about good and evil.
- C. S. Lewis, in the *Abolition of Man*, reports that versions of the Golden Rule, 'Do unto others as you would have them do unto you', are to be found in every tradition and culture worldwide.

These facts establish evidence that we were created as moral beings, designed for morality.

The birth of Isaac and the expulsion of Ishmael

God's original promise to Abraham now came to fruition.

- He opened Sarah's womb and, against all gynaecological odds, she gave birth to a child.
- The emphasis on this event in the text conveys the message that God delivers on his promises.
- His faithfulness needs constant emphasis to give us stability in the midst of life's uncertainties.

When the baby was weaned, there was a great feast of celebration.

But not all of the laughter would have pleased Sarah.

- She heard the teenage Ishmael, perhaps 15, laughing in mockery.
- In a fit of jealousy, she ordered Abraham to throw Hagar and her son out of the house.

She was not prepared for Ishmael to be a joint-heir with Isaac.

Abraham, who loved Ishmael, was deeply displeased. Indeed, he was angry.

- He had thrown Hagar out once on Sarah's order and God had sent her back.
- This time God intervened, telling Abraham to do as his wife requested.

Interestingly, the ancient Sumerian code of the time suggested that the freedom received was adequate compensation for the expulsion.

Abraham may have been encouraged in this by recalling that God had promised to make Ishmael a great nation.

- And in fact Josephus, the Roman-Jewish historian, regarded Ishmael as the father of the Arabs.
- And Muslims today identify Ishmael as an ancestor of Muhammad.

What about the compensation? Abraham certainly could have afforded to give her a monetary settlement.

- Apparently, he made no attempt to do so.

- He rose early in the morning, gave her bread and water,
- and sent her away, accompanied only by her son.

What were Abraham and Sarah thinking?

- Abraham was losing the son he had come to love.
- Sarah was delighted to get rid of the competition.

Mother and son walked out of the family life of Abraham and were gone.

New Testament insights

We have seen that the events of Genesis have been applied by Paul to Christian believers as spiritual offspring of Abraham.

- Isaac had been chosen by God to carry the seed project forward; Ishmael had not.
- Paul writes that Ishmael was born according to the flesh, and Isaac according to the Spirit.

God rescues Hagar and Ishmael

After being sent from Abraham's home

- Hagar and Ishmael's supplies were quickly exhausted; and
- Hagar left the boy under a bush and moved away, not wishing to watch him starve to death.

But God cared for Hagar and Ishmael. An angel called to Hagar, telling her

- not to be afraid;
- that God would make a great nation of Ishmael.

Looking up, Hagar saw a well of life-giving water, and her fears began to lift. God's attitude towards Hagar was very different from Sarah's.

The last we hear from Hagar and Ishmael is in Genesis 21.20–21.

- He grew up in the wilderness and became an expert hunter.
- His mother arranged for him to marry an Egyptian woman.

God was with him.

Sarah and Hagar in the New Testament

Paul writes in Galatians 4.23, 'But the son of the slave was born according to the flesh, while the son of the free woman was born through the promise.'

Paul is saying that these women represent two covenants. One covenant, given from Mount Sinai, bears children unto slavery.

- The Sinai covenant's children were people who tried to live according to the covenant's principles.
- Jewish believers lived under the terms and conditions of the Sinai covenant until Christ came.

And this is still true today for many from different religious backgrounds.

The biblical law of God has underpinned life in Europe and the West for centuries. We are warned of the danger of a shift in our moral base from the Judeo-Christian view, which incorporates:

- the ideals of freedom
- the autonomous conduct of life
- the individual morality of conscience
- human rights and democracy.

Attempts to keep the law, though well intentioned, cannot give us eternal life and God's acceptance.

The covenant at Sinai was not the law. It was a two-party agreement between God and the people based on the law. We are talking about an agreement with a holy God who cannot tolerate any level of transgression.

- So, if you want to base your relationship with him on keeping all his commands it has to be 100 per cent.
- This was impossible, but Israel thought they could do it. They had to find out by long, hard experience that they couldn't.

God provided a temporary solution of sacrifices to teach that sin needed to be atoned for, and revealed that a new covenant was needed.

Paul explains the seriousness of breaking the conditions of the covenant and why Christ had to die.

- 'Christ redeemed us from the curse of the law by becoming a curse for us' (Gal. 3.13).
- 'By works of the law no human being will be justified in his sight' (Rom. 3.20).

Many of Paul's fellow Jews rejected his message, as many people do today.

Mount Sinai and Jerusalem as metaphorical mothers

Paul argues that Hagar and Sarah represent two covenants:

- Hagar represents the covenant from Sinai, which corresponds to the Jerusalem that is now (in the time of Paul, in the first instance).
  - The Jerusalem of Paul's day had rejected Christ as the key to the eventual possession of the promised inheritance and based its hope on its own efforts to keep the law from Sinai.
- Sarah represents the unconditional covenant God made with Abraham, which corresponds to the Jerusalem that is above.
  - That Jerusalem is the vast community of Jews and Gentiles who are spiritual children of Abraham, who base their hope of eternal life on Jesus Christ.

Isaiah affirmed this two centuries before Paul's day (Isa. 51.1–2).

Abraham swears an oath to Abimelech

Abimelech next approached Abraham with a request to make a non-aggression pact between them and their descendants. The pact would secure their mutual futures.

As we look back over Abraham's life, we can discern just how much God had been faithful to his promise to shield him. If Abraham had understood this, he might not have been so concerned about security.

- Fear and anxiety are very real.
- Confidence in the love and care of God can overturn fear and anxiety.

Jesus dedicated part of the Sermon on the Mount to the question of security.

- He gave a principle regarding wealth accumulation.
- Investment is a good idea – provided that it is investment in the world to come.

Jesus also addressed in the Sermon on the Mount what should be our motivation for work.

- No one can serve two masters. You cannot serve God and money.
- Serving God is the key to conquering fear.

Jesus' answer to anxiety is to seek God's rule in our lives.

- Abram's insecurity grew deeper and lasted longer than was really necessary.
- In contrast, Paul's trust in God was not dependent on the level of his worldly security.

The tendency to trust the gift rather than the Giver has sadly characterized individual believers as well as churches.

Application questions

1. Abraham did not waste time before resuming his ploy of telling others that his wife Sarah was his sister. He had apparently forgotten or not believed God's promise to him in Genesis 15 to be his shield. Can Abraham be defended in this?
2. When called on by Abimelech to give his motives, Abraham replied that he felt there was no fear of God in Gerar. Why was he wrong?
3. When Isaac was weaned, there was a big celebration. Everyone seemed to be making merry and enjoying the occasion, including Ishmael, who was a teenager at the time. In a fit of jealousy, Sarah ordered Abraham to throw him and his mother out of the house. Was she trusting God to turn this to good?
4. What do you make of Abraham's provision of compensation for Hagar? He could certainly have afforded to set her up in another place, ensuring her safety and that of Ishmael. Yet he ushered them away with some bread and water. He was within the law, but it looks heartless. What do you think?
5. Now we come to the important moral of the story. In Paul's time there was tension in some churches regarding how a person could be justified before God. Some said it was by keeping the law; others that it was by faith in God through Christ. Explain how the Hagar/Ishmael and Sarah/Isaac story clarifies this.
6. The biblical law of God has underpinned life in the West for centuries. But there has been a shift in our moral base from the Judeo-Christian view to a postmodern relativist view. Can you cite some evidence for this from your current experience? What can we do to counter the trend?

15
God tests Abraham

One of the most famous stories, unique in world literature, now begins, 'After these things . . .' Abraham is commanded by God to sacrifice Isaac.

- He was a precious gift of God and required Abraham and Sarah to provide for his survival.
- There was a real danger here: was Abraham's trust shifting from Giver to gift – from God who gave Isaac to him, to Isaac exclusively?

We are informed in Scripture of the reason God tests people:

> And you shall remember the whole way that the LORD your God has led you these forty years in the wilderness, that he might humble you, testing you to know what was in your heart, whether you would keep his commandments or not (Deut. 8.2)

Abraham's test came when God addressed him.

- Using his name for the first and only time in Scripture, God said: 'Take . . . your only son Isaac, whom you love, and go to the land of Moriah, and offer him there as a burnt offering.'
- Moriah was a mountain range in Israel, where the city of Jerusalem was eventually situated and where Solomon would build the Temple.
- Abraham had already 'sacrificed' one son, Ishmael, by sending him away.
- Now to hear God command him to kill Isaac must have shaken Abraham to the core of his being.

Would God command a human sacrifice?

- The practice was carried out by adherents of Molech, the Ammonite god, but this is roundly condemned in the Bible in Leviticus 20.1–5.
- We observe that God did not allow Abraham to sacrifice Isaac. God is wholly against human sacrifices.

To offer Isaac as a burnt offering indicated that Isaac was given entirely to God. Moses would later institute daily burnt offerings expressing Israel's offering of itself completely to God.

This is reflected in Jesus' summary of the greatest commandment, 'You shall love the Lord your God

- with all your heart
- and with all your soul
- and with all your mind
- and with all your strength.'

And the second is, 'You shall love your neighbour as yourself' (Mark 12.30–31). This amounts to more than all burnt offerings.

We do not read of any verbal response from Abraham at God's command. There is neither protesting, nor pleading for Isaac's life. Is this evidence of his ongoing belief that the Judge of all the earth would do right?

The philosopher Kierkegaard thought that it was reason itself that Abraham was being asked to sacrifice[29] since there was a complete contradiction between

- God blessing the world through Isaac; and
- God demanding that he be killed as a sacrifice.

However, Abraham knew that God was able to raise Isaac from the dead in order to fulfil his promise.

Criticism of God's command to Abraham has typically come from those whose worldview is naturalistic. They deny any supernatural dimension to life. Hence, to them, terminating life is unqualified evil.

John Calvin wrote:

> God does not require him to put his son immediately to death, but compels him to revolve this execution in his mind during three

> whole days, that in preparing to sacrifice his son, he may still more severely torture all his own senses. (Institutes 565).[30]

Abraham instructed the two men he took with them to wait while they worshipped, and promised that they would return. His faith

- had assured him that God could raise the dead;
- had convinced him that he and Isaac would return.

As they ascended the mountain, Isaac with the wood on his back was like a 'condemned man carrying his own cross'. Centuries later, Jesus would go out 'bearing his own cross'.

- Isaac had no choice.
- Jesus had a choice.

The story casts a mighty shadow over subsequent history. Where is the Lamb?

- 'Behold, the Lamb of God, who takes away the sin of the world!' (John 1.29).
- 'Like a lamb that is led to the slaughter, and like a sheep that before its shearers is silent, so he opened not his mouth' (Isa. 53.7).
- 'A Lamb standing, as though it had been slain' (Rev. 5.6).

What was Isaac's reaction to these events?

- He could easily have outrun or overpowered Abraham, but he didn't. Was he terrified, or did he trust God to provide? We do not know.
- He may have asked, 'Why have you forsaken me?' as a great Son of a greater Father would do one day from a cross erected on Mount Moriah.

The silence was broken by a voice that called to Abraham, saying:

- 'Do not lay your hand on the boy or do anything to him,

for now I know that you fear God, seeing that you have not withheld your son . . . from me.'

A burnt offering was still necessary. Abraham found a ram and offered it up.

- A burnt offering instead of his son
- An instance of substitutionary atonement.

This principle reaches its full expression in the death of Christ in our place (Mark 10.45).

This was the second time the call of an angel saved the life of one of Abraham's children.

- An angel called to Hagar to lift up Ishmael.
- An angel called to Abraham not to lay a hand to Isaac.

Both occasions involved the saving of life. Abraham loved both boys. So did God.

Shadows of the cross

The New Testament uses Old Testament language to describe Jesus' death on the cross.

- Jesus is the Lamb of God that takes away the sin of the world.
- Jesus came to give his life a ransom for many.
- Jesus shed his blood and gave his body for us.

The story of Abraham and Isaac is deep, their psychological pain unimaginable. The story of the cross is immeasurably deeper.

- 'He who did not spare his own Son but gave him up for us all . . .'
- Abraham called the name of the place 'the Lord will provide'.

Justification by works

Whatever the implications of God's foreknowledge and omniscience,

- he insists that we gain knowledge by experience;
- he wants to see evidence that our faith is genuine.

The letter of James interprets this incident as illustrating the principle of justification by works. James makes it clear that Abraham's work did not earn him salvation.

- Abraham's faith was completed by his works.
- Abraham's works are evidence of genuine faith.

God was not finished with Abraham. The angel was called again to add a solemn oath to reinforce the original oath.

This oath endured through the centuries so that, when we get to the New Testament, we find both Mary, the mother of Jesus, and Zechariah, the father of John the Baptist, recalling it.

- Mary: 'He spoke to our fathers' (Luke 1.55).
- Zechariah: 'The oath that he swore to our father Abraham' (Luke 1.73).

The most important point in the oath for Mary and Zechariah was the freedom that allowed them to serve God without fear.

The aftermath

'The heart of the story . . . is the conversation between father and son as they went together up the mountain'.[31]

- It began with Isaac's question, 'Where is the lamb?'
- It ended with Abraham's answer, 'God will provide.'

Abraham taught Isaac to place his trust not in his faith, but in the Lord.

Application questions

1. In this passage, God commands Abraham to take his son Isaac to Mount Moriah and offer him as a sacrifice on an altar. How can this be? Would God really command someone to make a sacrifice of another human? Before reading the chapter, were you at all conflicted about the story? How so?
2. To offer Isaac as a burnt offering indicated that Isaac was given entirely to God. This is a very subtle point. Did you pick up on it? Do you see the difference between symbolic and actual in this scenario? Do you think that Abraham was counting on symbolism here or was this very real to him as he walked through these events?
3. Kierkegaard explains the situation as God asking Abraham to sacrifice his reason, since God had promised to bless the world through Isaac, and this could not happen if he had been sacrificed on an altar. Kierkegaard does not consider that God could do anything supernatural to bring the episode to a good end. In what respect was Kierkegaard wrong?
4. John Calvin's focus is on the duration of the stress on Abraham.[32] He writes that God doesn't demand that Abraham immediately slay Isaac, but lets the thoughts of what was coming torture his mind for the entire journey to Moriah. Do you agree? Give your reasons.
5. Finally God intervened: 'Do not lay your hand on the boy or do anything to him, for now I know that you fear God, seeing that you have not withheld your son . . . from me.' Do you think Abraham was able to connect all the dots at this point? What about the ram caught in the thicket?
6. Writing in the New Testament, James makes the statement that Abraham's faith was completed by his works. Those works were evidence that his faith was genuine. This is helpful. Explain how James's teaching contributes to our understanding of faith versus works.

16

Applying the Moriah experience

In more ways than one, Moriah represented the mountain top of Abraham's journey of faith. It teaches all of us important lessons about trusting God in the face of trials and suffering.

All believers will experience testing in their faith journey with God. The key consideration is the cost: the cost of obeying God, the cost of following Jesus and putting him first.

- Giving up a bad habit or something morally wrong is not a sacrifice.
- True sacrifice involves giving up something that is good, wholesome and right to put God first.
- Putting Jesus first and hating all else does not mean hating in a literal sense but in a comparative sense.

Each mountain-top experience is unique in its own way but all who experience them find that they ultimately reveal God's provision.

- As did Abraham and Isaac (discovering a ram caught by its horns in the thicket).
- As did a Siberian believer who underwent unspeakable persecution in the Gulag for his faith.
- As did Job at the hands of Satan testing his faith in God through the loss of his family, wealth and friends.

The problem of evil and suffering, much of it caused by human beings, drives many people to atheism.

- The story of Moriah underscores the suffering of the Lord Jesus on the cross.

- The cross communicates that God in Jesus entered into pain and suffering.

The resurrection of Jesus from the tomb gives us a sure and certain hope, which is the birthright of every believer in Christ. But it doesn't remove sorrow at the loss of a loved one. We sorrow, but not as those who have no hope.

Our lives on earth are transient. The Lord will provide until our journey on earth is done.

Application questions

1. All believers will experience testing in their faith journey with God. Some experience more hardship and suffering than others. Do you know of some believers who are rarely tested? Do you know of others who have a full plate? Are you remembering them in your prayers?
2. All followers of Jesus are asked to confirm the genuineness of their faith by their actions and behaviour. Can you cite a specific example from your own experience? What is the difference between this and salvation by works?
3. Sacrifice involves giving up something that is good, wholesome and right in order to put God first. Can you give some examples? What about charitable giving? Does the principle apply here?
4. Can you give an example of God's provision in your walk with him? How do you know that it was from God? How did Abraham and Isaac know that the ram was a provision from God?
5. Many people are put off by what is known as the problem of evil and suffering. 'If God is all-powerful,' they say, 'why does he allow evil and suffering?' Why do you think we have diseases and calamities? Why doesn't he just exterminate evil and pain and let us live without such troubles?
6. 'The Lord will provide' is a recurring theme in Scripture. Do you find that comforting? Can you cite some Scripture passages that illustrate God's providence?

Part 5

GENESIS 22.20—25.11

17
Lessons from the life of Sarah

The focus of the narrative now shifts to the business of finding a bride for Isaac, the promised seed.

- Abraham was informed about what had been happening in Mesopotamia.
- The news was important for obvious reasons – it concerned developments in Abraham's family in Haran.

The death of Sarah

Sarah died at the age of 127. Abraham certainly missed her greatly. They had had a long journey together.

Abraham considered it important to have a burial site for Sarah and his family. His negotiations with the Hittites provide some subtle points that warrant elaboration.

- The terms 'sojourner' and 'foreigner' mean 'resident alien' and would later be used by Peter to describe Christian believers.
- Abraham wanted to buy the land. He wanted to possess it in perpetuity. He would not bury his wife with the Canaanites.
- The dialogue bears all the marks of authenticity. Similar negotiations take place routinely in that part of the world.
- The price of the property was greatly inflated. We are given two other purchase prices for comparison.
- The mention of trees accords with the Hittite practice of listing the number of trees on a property, adding authenticity.

Here is a summary of some of the lessons we learn from Sarah's life in the book of Genesis.

- Sarah is mentioned more often than any other woman in Scripture. Three New Testament references are important.
  - Romans 9.9: God promised her a son within the year.
  - Hebrews 11.11: she believed God's promise to her.
  - 1 Peter 3.6: she obeyed Abraham, calling him lord.
- The third of these passages has caused questions, especially when viewed in the larger context of marriage. Sarah is held up as an example of what it means to be a good wife, even though
  - she was sometimes not exactly pure;
  - she was far from respectful;
  - she had a fiery temper;
  - she sometimes bossed Abraham around;
  - some of her decisions lacked moral clarity.

Biblical teaching on marital relationships often comes under attack as old-fashioned, sexist and misogynistic. Many say that it is a dominant male-centred power narrative that needs to be set aside after centuries of being unchallenged. How can we answer such charges?

- Being old does not imply being old-fashioned. The definition of marriage in Genesis is used in the New Testament.
- Jesus and Paul, many centuries later, were both concerned with the status of women.
  - Jesus treated women with great respect and defended them when they were maligned.
  - Women were given prominence by the Gospel writers as the first witnesses of the resurrection.
  - Paul was honoured to have women as his fellow workers, for example Lydia in Philippi and Priscilla in Corinth.

Genesis 1.26 is a principle for the basis of civilized life that gives dignity and value to human beings – God made both men and women in his image as companions for each other, standing side by side, with neither inferior to the other but complementing each other.

What is meant by Paul's injunction that wives should submit to their husbands (Eph. 5.22–23)?

- The marriage metaphor is illustrated by the phrase 'one body, one flesh, one spirit'.
  - The marriage relationship is an experience of surrender without absorption, service without compulsion and love without condition.

Is it degrading, disparaging or insulting to women to say that within the marriage relationship man is the head of the woman and the wife must submit to her husband?

- The man has a head – Christ himself.
- Christ has a Head – the Lord God.
- The Trinity is a hierarchy of equals and we can apply that to other Christian relationships.
- We practise all kinds of hierarchies of equals in our lives.

How can Scripture hold Sarah out as a paradigm of godly behaviour?

- Genesis is a series of snapshots of Sarah's behaviour – short clips over her whole lifetime.
- We see a wonderful pattern of hospitality during her and Abraham's lifetimes.
- People change. The arrival of her child Isaac must have relieved some pressure, allowing her to change in good ways.
- Even in what we would describe as exemplary marriages, there can be times of friction and unpleasantness.

Husbands are not always right. God told Abraham so.

We can imagine that, as in many marriages, times of stress and failure were soon forgotten as life settled down to a more normal routine, hopefully with God in a much more central role in the family.

Application questions

1 Finding a suitable burial place for Sarah's body now became an urgent matter for Abraham. People tend to let the significant end-of-life questions slide, addressing them at the last possible moment.

In addition to the burial details, there are other significantly more important decisions to be addressed. What are these? Have you addressed them?

2 Abraham's negotiations with the Hittites for a burial site are interesting. Do you think they give credence to the authenticity of the narrative? Everyone involved was playing things close to their chest. Why was this?
3 Many today find the biblical teaching about different roles for husbands and wives problematic, while others find that it works. Do you have a view either way?
4 Paul's injunction that wives should submit to their husbands is a case in point (Eph. 5.22–23). Many find this difficult. Yet it is explained as 'an experience of surrender without absorption, service without compulsion and love without condition'. What do you think about this explanation?

18
A bride for the promised seed

Just after receiving the promise that his offspring would be as the sand of the sea, Abraham received a message from Mesopotamia about his brother Nahor's family. It made specific mention of Nahor's daughter Rebekah.

Abraham then entrusted his most faithful servant with the mission of finding a wife for Isaac.

- He made the servant promise not to look among the local Canaanite women.
- He told the servant to journey to Abraham's relatives in Mesopotamia to find someone.

Guess who!

The servant expressed concern that a woman might not be prepared to make such a journey. Abraham informed him:

- 'the LORD, the God of heaven . . . will send his angel before you';
- 'you shall take a wife for my son from there';
- 'if the woman is not willing to follow you, then you will be free from this oath'.

Abraham desired a wife for Isaac who had the same kind of spirit he and Sarah did in making their original journey.

Abraham did not want under any circumstances to allow Isaac to go to Mesopotamia.

- Why was this? Did Abraham sense some weakness in Isaac?
- He felt that, if a woman came to them in Canaan, there was little likelihood she (or Isaac) would leave.

Here is an important lesson for younger believers, as they seek a life partner:

- to look for someone who is committed, like them;
- to make a clean break with the past and journey with the Lord.

As the caravan headed to Haran, Abraham's servant prayed that the Lord would lead him to the right woman:

- that she would offer him water;
- that she would also water his camels.

His approach was thoughtfully designed to reveal the character of the young woman, especially with regard to hospitality.

- Hospitality is an important biblical virtue.
- Hospitality to strangers was regarded as a sacred duty.
- Hospitality was repeatedly praised and encouraged by Jesus and the apostles.

This servant was certainly a wise man and a good judge of human character. Rebekah arrived as he was praying.

- When the servant asked her for a drink of water, she replied: 'Drink, my lord,' and gave him water.
- When he'd finished, she offered to water the camels and made multiple trips.

So she passed the servant's hospitality test with flying colours.

When he asked her whose daughter she was and if her father could accommodate them for the night, she answered that she was Bethuel's daughter and that there was room for them and for the camels.

Rebekah then ran ahead to her home, leaving the caravan behind to follow.

- She told her family everything that had happened with the servant.
- Her brother Laban ran out to meet the servant and invited them to stay.

The servant accompanied Laban to the house and then told the story of his mission.

- He told them the exploits of Abraham and Sarah and their son Isaac.
- He shared with them Isaac's need for a wife and the story of his meeting Rebekah at the well.
- He also described in detail his prayer to God, asking him to lead him to the right person and confirm that choice.

Rebekah's family, seeing the hand of God in leading the servant to Rebekah, gave permission for her to go to Isaac with the servant. What convinced Rebekah to go?

- First, the gifts indicating that her future in-laws were wealthy and generous.
- Second, the fact that they had shared kinship – they were already family.
- Third, the story of Abraham and Isaac's life and the servant's story of his mission.

All these things convinced her that this was an exciting direction for her life.

The servant revealed to the potential bride the wealth and glory of the son, with the result that she was prepared to embark on the journey to Canaan to marry him.

A very similar narrative at a much higher level is the story of God the Father in heaven

- sending his Spirit to witness to his Son by revealing his glory and attracting people to take a faith journey with him;
- equipping the disciples of Jesus to take this same message to their world, making disciples in all nations.

Hence, in a real sense, this story is a prototype of how we can show the glory of Jesus to people who will put their trust in him and become Abraham's children by faith.

Many of us have opportunities, sometimes in other countries, to see God's Spirit open hearts and minds to receive Jesus as Saviour and make the greatest step of all.

Cities and their foundations

We, a part of the Church, will participate in an indescribably glorious wedding, the marriage supper of the Lamb. We shall have reached the city Abraham sought:

- the city called the New Jerusalem and the bride of the Lamb;
- the city contrasted in Revelation with Babylon the Great, a city on earth that is a prostitute.

Abraham was called to leave Babylon and its many gods to live a life of trust in God. His narrative comes to an end with a repetition of his call, this time to a young woman to

- leave the region Abraham had left;
- become the bride of a man she had never seen;
- live for the city whose builder and maker is God.

Some important principles for living our lives come from this beautiful account.

- We need to pray for our children and grandchildren, that God will give them suitable life partners if he wants them to be married.
- We need to be willing to leave home to discover and develop what God intends for our lives.

Our goal is not this world. We seek the city where Abraham has already been with God for centuries.

Application questions

1 How do you think Abraham's servant did in carrying out the affairs of his master faithfully, relying on God for direction and success in the important responsibility Abraham had given him? Explain your thinking.

2 A lesson from this story, for believers who do not choose the single life, is the importance of finding a life partner who is committed to journeying with the Lord. Unfortunately, some people don't give enough thought to choosing a life partner and the results can be catastrophic. It was of the highest importance to Abraham that Isaac's wife should share his faith. Is this still an important consideration for believers? Explain your position.
3 It is especially impressive that Abraham's servant was praying about the situation when he arrived at the well in Haran. Many people, upon reading this account, would chalk up the outcomes to coincidence. Have you ever experienced this kind of 'coincidence' yourself? What persuades you that it was more than a coincidence?
4 What do you think of the servant giving Rebekah a gold ring and bracelets? Was he trying to bribe her to get her to come back to Canaan with him? Do you think Rebekah would be persuaded by expensive gifts? We are told that the reason for these gifts was to communicate that Abraham, Sarah and Isaac were significant people. What do you think?
5 We need to be willing to 'leave home', so to speak, in order to discover what God intends for our lives. Do you have any stories along these lines that you could share?
6 Finally, our goal is not this world. We seek the city where Abraham has been with God for centuries. Are you seeking that city? What are some of the things you are doing that would communicate that you are on the road?

19

The last days of Abraham – and beyond

After Abraham's servant returned to Canaan with Rebekah, Isaac brought her to his mother's tent, and then they were married.

- Rebekah comforted Isaac on the death of his mother.
- Later, Abraham married a woman named Keturah.
- Over the ensuing years, Abraham and Keturah would have six sons together.

In his later years, Abraham gave gifts to these sons and sent them off to the east.

- He gave his vast fortune to Isaac.
- He lived to be 175 and died after a good life.
- His sons Isaac and Ishmael buried him in the cave of Machpelah, where Sarah was buried.
- God blessed Ishmael with 12 sons, but tension between Isaac and Ishmael remained.

God had promised Abraham that he would bring blessing to the nations of the world. Jesus, speaking to the religious leaders in Matthew 22.31–32, quoted the words of God to Moses at the burning bush: 'I am the God of Abraham, and the God of Isaac, and the God of Jacob.'

- This implies that the story of Abraham was not terminated by his physical death.

Abraham brought the blessing of faith to the world.

Another example of the blessing Abraham brought is seen in the story of the centurion who asked Jesus to heal his servant (Matt. 8.10–12).

- The centurion told Jesus he did not need to come to him. He could just say the word and the servant would be healed.
- Jesus was impressed with the Gentile's faith and noted that many Gentiles would come to faith because of his example.

The story of the rich man and Lazarus illustrates how Jews who never repented of their evil deeds nor trusted God will see Abraham.

- Lazarus died and was carried to Abraham's side.
- The rich man died and asked Abraham to send Lazarus to minister to him and send someone to warn his brothers.
- In the parable, Abraham responded that if they didn't hear Moses and the prophets, they would not be convinced if someone should rise from the dead.

Some suggest that this story was a real event, not a parable.[33] And it illustrates the teaching of Jesus that there will be rewards for faithful stewardship in this life.

- Abraham had been wealthy and generous in life.
- The rich man had been selfish and ignored God and Lazarus.

Abraham was chosen to communicate a vital lesson to everyone: people do not need to be convinced of an afterlife; they need to be convinced that their neglect of God's law is serious enough to consign them to hell.

We conclude the story of Abraham, listening to him plead with us to take the word of God seriously and to bring it to bear on a world that desperately needs it. What will our reaction be?

- Will we prove to be true and genuine children of Abraham, standing firm in our faith in Christ, spending time and energy to know God's word and take it to the world?

- Will we invest our energy in learning how to explain that message to the next generation of believers to empower them to resist secularism, relativism and atheism?
- Is the eternal city which Abraham sought, a living, vital prospect for us? Are we building its principles of faith in the unseen God into our lives?

Abraham is one of the cloud of many witnesses who encourage us to look to Jesus and to run the race eagerly saying, 'Amen. Come, Lord Jesus!'

Lech lecha! Get going!

Application questions

1 God certainly delivered on his promise to bless the world through Abraham. Can you summarize how? Has Abraham blessed you as you have studied his life as a friend of God? Would you share some of the ways?

2 Abraham himself communicates a powerful message to Jewish people (and Gentiles also) in the parable/story of the rich man and Lazarus. He told the rich man that, if people wouldn't believe Moses and the prophets, they wouldn't be convinced even if someone were to rise from the dead. Does that attitude remind you at all of our times today? Jesus rose from the dead. The evidence is incontrovertible! Does this motivate you? How?

3 At the end of the book we are asked what our reaction will be. Will we take the message to the world? To the next generation? Will we build the principles of the city that Abraham sought into our lives? Will you do these things?

Notes

1 The Online Etymology Dictionary: Old English *freond* 'one attached to another by feelings of personal regard and preference', from Proto-Germanic *frijōjands* 'lover, friend' (source also of Old Norse *frændi*, Old Danish *frynt*, Old Frisian *friund*, Dutch *vriend*, Middle High German *friunt*, German *Freund*, Gothic *frijonds* 'friend'), from Proto-Indo European *priy-ont-*, 'loving', present participle form of root, *pri-* 'to love'.

2 Colin Hemer, *The Book of Acts in the Setting of Hellenistic History* (Tübingen: J. C. B. Mohr, 1989).

3 Peter J. Williams, *Can We Trust the Gospels?* (Grand Rapids, MI: Crossway, 2018).

4 Alan Millard, *Treasures from Bible Times* (Tring: Lion, 1985), p. 59.

5 Kenneth Kitchen, *On the Reliability of the Old Testament* (Grand Rapids, MI: Eerdmans, 2003), pp. 364–8.

6 R. K. Harrison, *Introduction to the Old Testament* (Grand Rapids, MI: Eerdmans, 1969), p. 112.

7 A. R. Millard and D. J. Wiseman (eds), *Essays on the Patriarchal Narratives* (Leicester: Inter-Varsity Press, 1980).

8 Leon Kass, *The Beginning of Wisdom: Reading Genesis* (Chicago, IL: University of Chicago Press, 2006), pp. 18–19.

9 Aristotle, *The Politics*, trans. T. A. Sinclair, revised and re-presented by Trevor J. Saunders (London: Penguin, 1992), 1253a7.

10 Jacques Ellul, *The Meaning of the City* (Grand Rapids, MI: Eerdmans, 1970), p. 16.

11 Philip Nobel, 'Lust for Height', American Enterprise Institute, 23 February 2007, available at: www.aei.org/articles/lust-for-height/ (accessed 3 May 2023).

12 C. S. Lewis, *That Hideous Strength*, The Cosmic Trilogy (London: Bodley Head, 1989).

13 Jonathan Haidt, 'Why the past ten years of American life have been uniquely stupid', *The Atlantic*, 11 April 2022.

14 Russell Moore, 'Fragmentation is not what's killing us', *Christianity Today*, 21 April 2022.
15 Yuval Noah Harari, *Homo Deus: A brief history of tomorrow* (London: Vintage, 2017).
16 C. S. Lewis, *That Hideous Strength*, The Cosmic Trilogy (London: Bodley Head, 1989).
17 G. Roux, *Ancient Iraq* (London: Penguin, 1992).
18 Kitchen, *On the Reliability of the Old Testament* pp. 358–9.
19 Available at: https://rabbisacks.org/covenant-conversation-5768-lechlecha-the-heroism-of-ordinary-life (accessed 6 May 2023).
20 Kass, *The Beginning of Wisdom*, p. 263.
21 Jonathan Sacks, *The Great Partnership* (London: Hodder & Stoughton, 2011), p. 8.
22 Sacks, *The Great Partnership*, p. 8.
23 See: www.cardus.ca/comment/article/forging-a-people-sustaining-a-nation/?mc_cid=2f66d06550&mc_eid=19b161f5a7 (accessed 21 March 2023).
24 Kass, *The Beginning of Wisdom*, p. 275.
25 Kass, *The Beginning of Wisdom*, p. 266.
26 Bertrand Russell, *Human Society in Ethics and Politics* (London: Allen and Unwin, 1954).
27 Richard Dawkins, *The Selfish Gene* (Oxford: Oxford University Press, 1976), p. 330.
28 Ros Clarke, *Forty Women: Unseen women of the Bible from Eden to Easter* (London: Inter-Varsity Press, 2021), p. 5.
29 Søren Kierkegaard, *Fear and Trembling* [*Frygt og Bæven*], 1843.
30 John Calvin, *Institutes*, I.565.
31 Kass, *The Beginning of Wisdom*, p. 359.
32 Calvin, *Institutes*, I.565.
33 For instance, parables do not give the names of people. See also David Gooding, *According to Luke: The third Gospel's ordered historical narrative* (Belfast: Myrtlefield House, 2013), p. 291, footnote 3.

Milton Keynes UK
Ingram Content Group UK Ltd.
UKHW022031191223
434673UK00009B/392